The History of Passenger Transport in Portsmouth

FARES PLEASE

Eric Watts

Published by Milestone Publications
62 Murray Road, Horndean,
Portsmouth, Hants. PO8 9JL

Design Brian Iles

Typeset by The Monitor, Hayling Island, Hampshire

Printed and Bound in Great Britain by
R.J. Acford, Industrial Estate, Chichester, Sussex

Cover Printed by
Conifer Press, Fareham, Hampshire

British Library Cataloguing in Publication Data
Watts, Eric
Fares please: the history of passenger transport in Portsmouth.
1. Local transit—England—Portsmouth (Hampshire)—History
I. Title
380.5′22′09422792 HE4719.P/

ISBN 0-903852-98-5

Author

After leaving school, Eric Watts became an apprentice with Chesterfield Corporation Transport. Two years after completing his training, he took a job repairing fork lift trucks, cars and lorries at a cardboard box factory.

By July 1966, he was once more working in transport as an Engineering Assistant for Halifax Corporation. On January 1st 1968, he was appointed as the Assistant Engineer with Oldham Corporation Transport. A major reorganisation of public transport in the Greater Manchester area in 1969 brought promotion to Eric again when he became District Engineer for the Oldham District of Greater Manchester Transport.

Eric Watts moved to Portsmouth in 1975 when he became Chief Engineer for the City of Portsmouth Passenger Transport Department. When Portsmouth City Transport Ltd. was formed in October 1986, marking the end of an era, Eric became Engineering Director for the new company.

This book celebrates the years of public transport in Portsmouth under the city department. The author spent three years researching, reading council minutes, publications by local historians, old newspaper cuttings and an office diary which recorded important events affecting the department between 1901 and 1939.

Eric's experiences, both on the shop floor and in management, gives him a great understanding and affection for the industry. He especially enjoyed talking to retired employees and recording many amusing anecdotes of former drivers and conductors.

Eric Watts is married with three children and lives in Drayton.

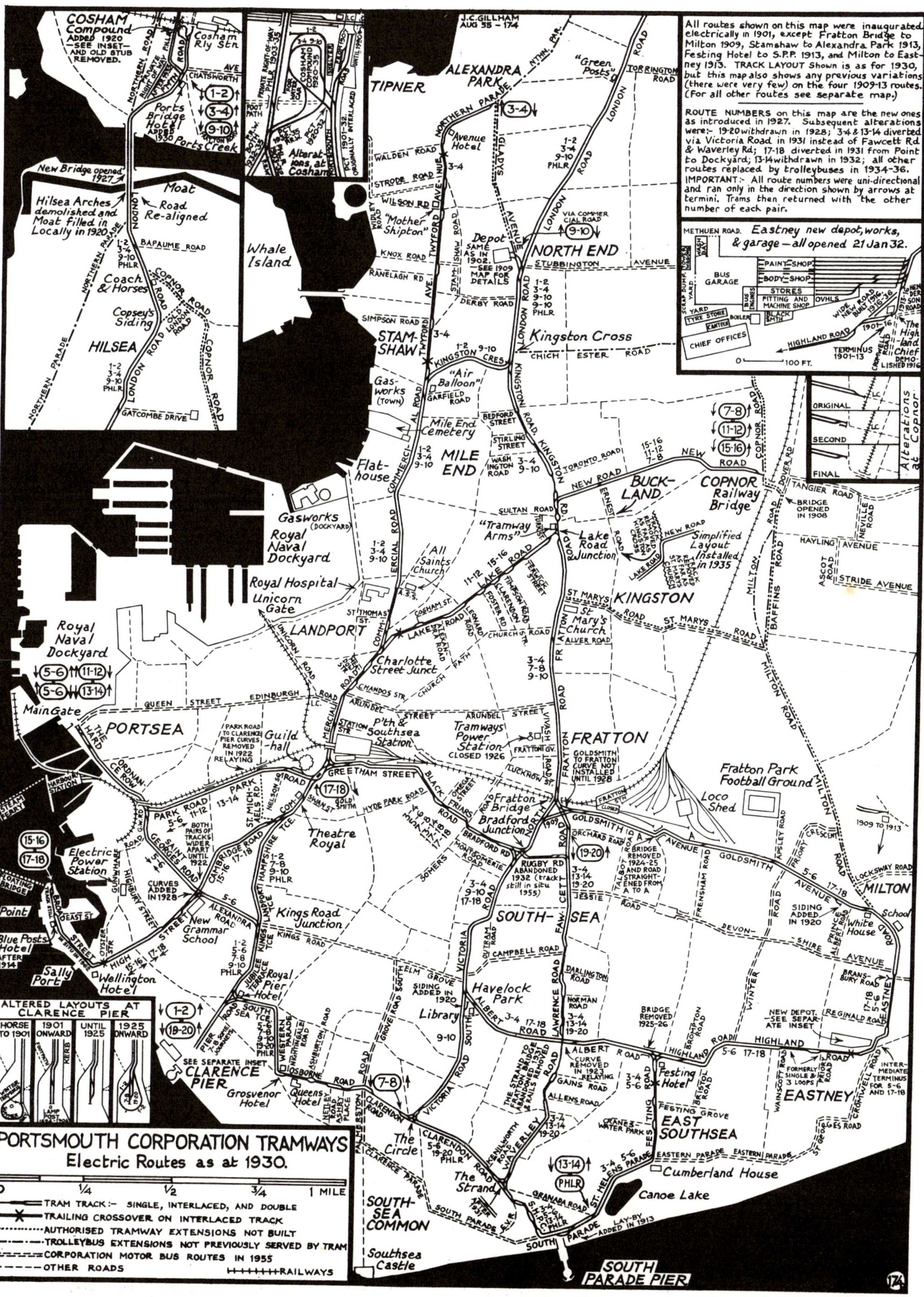

PORTSMOUTH CORPORATION TRAMWAYS
Electric Routes as at 1930.
0 1/4 1/2 3/4 1 MILE
TRAM TRACK:- SINGLE, INTERLACED, AND DOUBLE
TRAILING CROSSOVER ON INTERLACED TRACK
AUTHORISED TRAMWAY EXTENSIONS NOT BUILT
TROLLEYBUS EXTENSIONS NOT PREVIOUSLY SERVED BY TRAM
CORPORATION MOTOR BUS ROUTES IN 1955
OTHER ROADS
RAILWAYS
J.C. GILLHAM AUG 55 - 174
All routes shown on this map were inaugurated electrically in 1901, except Fratton Bridge to Milton 1909, Stamshaw to Alexandra Park 1913, Festing Hotel to S.P.P. 1913, and Milton to Eastney 1913. TRACK LAYOUT shown is as for 1930, but this map also shows any previous variations (there were very few) on the four 1909-13 routes. (For all other routes see separate map.)
ROUTE NUMBERS on this map are the new ones as introduced in 1927. Subsequent alterations were:- 19-20 withdrawn in 1928; 3-4 & 13-14 diverted via Victoria Road in 1931 instead of Fawcett Rd & Waverley Rd; 17-18 diverted in 1931 from Point to Dockyard; 13-14 withdrawn in 1932; all other routes replaced by trolleybuses in 1934-36.
IMPORTANT:- All route numbers were uni-directional and ran only in the direction shown by arrows at termini. Trams then returned with the other number of each pair.
Eastney new depot, works, & garage – all opened 21 Jan 32.
METHUEN ROAD.
BUS GARAGE
PAINT SHOP
BODY SHOP
STORES
FITTING AND MACHINE SHOP
TYRE STORE
CANTEEN
BOILER
BLACK SMITH
CHIEF OFFICES
HIGHLAND ROAD
TERMINUS 1901-13
The High-land Chief DEMOLISHED 1916
100 FT.
Alterations at Copnor
ORIGINAL
SECOND
FINAL
COSHAM Compound ADDED 1920 – SEE INSET – AND OLD STUB REMOVED.
Cosham Rly Stn
Ports Bridge Hotel ADDED 1930
Ports Creek
Alterations at Cosham
New Bridge opened 1927
Moat
Hilsea Arches demolished and Moat filled in Locally in 1920
Road Re-aligned
Coach & Horses
Copsey's Siding
HILSEA
GATCOMBE DRIVE
Whale Island
TIPNER
ALEXANDRA PARK
"Green Posts"
Avenue Hotel
"Mother Shipton"
Depot SAME AS IN 1902. SEE 1909 MAP FOR DETAILS
NORTH END
STAMSHAW
Kingston Cross
"Air Balloon"
Gasworks (TOWN)
Mile End Cemetery
MILE END
Flathouse
Gasworks (DOCKYARD)
Royal Naval Dockyard
Royal Hospital
Unicorn Gate
LANDPORT
"Tramway Arms"
All Saints Church
BUCKLAND
COPNOR Railway Bridge
BRIDGE OPENED IN 1908
Lake Road Junction
Simplified Layout Installed in 1935
KINGSTON
St Mary's Church
Charlotte Street Junct
Main Gate
PORTSEA
Guildhall
P'th & Southsea Station
Tramways Power Station CLOSED 1926
FRATTON
GOLDSMITH TO FRATTON CURVE NOT INSTALLED UNTIL 1928
Fratton Park Football Ground
Loco Shed
Fratton Bridge
Bradford Junction
Theatre Royal
Electric Power Station
CURVES ADDED IN 1928
Point
Blue Posts Hotel AFTER 1914
Sally Port
Wellington Hotel
New Grammar School
Kings Road Junction
RUGBY RD ABANDONED 1932 (track still in situ 1955)
BRIDGE REMOVED 1924-25 AND ROAD STRAIGHTENED FROM A TO A
SOUTHSEA
MILTON
SIDING ADDED IN 1920
White House
Havelock Park
SIDING ADDED IN 1920
Library
Royal Pier Hotel
ALTERED LAYOUTS AT CLARENCE PIER
HORSE TO 1901
1901 ONWARD
UNTIL 1925
1925 ONWARD
SEE SEPARATE INSET CLARENCE PIER
Grosvenor Hotel
Queens Hotel
The Circle
BRIDGE REMOVED 1925-26
Festing Hotel
CURVE REMOVED IN 1923 RELAYING
NEW DEPOT. SEE SEPARATE INSET
FORMERLY SINGLE & 3 LOOPS
INTERMEDIATE TERMINUS FOR 5-6 AND 17-18
EASTNEY
EAST SOUTHSEA
Cumberland House
Canoe Lake
The Strand
SOUTHSEA COMMON
Southsea Castle
LAY-BY ADDED IN 1913
SOUTH PARADE PIER
174

CONTENTS

ACKNOWLEDGEMENTS

It would have been impossible to write this book without the help of many people. I must, first, acknowledge my wife, Valerie, for typing the original manuscript and tolerating the taking over of her cupboards for my voluminous reference material.

The work of several local transport historians has been extremely useful. The late S.E. Harrison's book *Tramways of Portsmouth*, A.F. Milton and L. Bern's *History of Portsmouth Transport 1840 - 1977*, and Leslie Bern's catalogue of events taken from council minutes and local newspapers has proved invaluable.

Many retired members of the department have related interesting events, most of which I have mentioned in the manuscript. I am especially grateful to Miss J. Spaven, the granddaughter of a former general manager, who worked for many years as secretary to Mr. Ben Hall and all successive managers; and to Mr. C. Phillips who worked for the department for more than 30 years.

The City of Portsmouth Passenger Transport Department and the City Archivist have been most helpful in the provision of photographs. Many bus enthusiasts have loaned me photographs, and I thank L. Bern, T. Dethridge, P. Couper, J. Dorey, A. Lambert and the Southdown Enthusiasts Club for their help. Portsmouth and Sunderland Newspapers p.l.c. has kindly provided photographs from *The News* archives and reports from newspaper cuttings were most useful.

Information about the Portsdown and Horndean Light Railway was confirmed by Mr. Pethybridge, a local historian who has a wealth of knowledge on the subject.

The maps of the tramway, trolley bus routes and the Portsdown and Horndean Light Railway are reproduced by kind permission of Mr. J.C.Gillham who prepared the maps originally for Harrison's *Tramways of Portsmouth*.

Last, but by no means least, I must thank the current and former employees of the City of Portsmouth Passenger Transport Department for their assistance in the preparation of this book.

FOREWORD

EIGHTY-FIVE years is a long time. Eighty-five years in the 20th Century have proved sufficient to produce sweeping social, economic and technological change.

The Portsmouth of 1901 was, in many ways, a different place from the Portsmouth of 1986. Even so, someone living in the city 85 years ago who surveyed the urban scene today would recognise at least one significant feature — vehicles owned by the Municipal Public Transport Undertaking plying the streets, busily engaged in carrying people around the City.

The vehicles may have changed but the function has endured. Day in, day out, in fair weather and foul, in good times and in bad, in war and in peace the men and women of the Municipal Transport Department have endeavoured to provide a vital public service.

The efforts have not always been appreciated! Services have sometimes failed to go where some residents thought they should. Some services have been actively opposed. Fares have never been low enough and frequencies have never been sufficient; more often than not, political and public debates have raged on the subject. Is public transport a social service or a commercial activity?

Through it all, however, countless millions of passenger journeys have been successfully accomplished and the most difficult and valuable of all cargoes delivered successfully to their destinations.

In this book Eric Watts has captured much of the fascinating story of Portsmouth City Council's involvement in public transport operation.

The timing is opportune. The council ceased to operate public transport services directly at midnight on October 25, 1986, and handed over the function to Portsmouth City Transport Ltd. It is the end of another proud chapter in the city's history and I hope that this book will be a fitting reminder of the 85 years of dedication and sheer hard work which has underlined the success of the municipal passenger transport department and that it will encourage the future generations who, undoubtedly, will be providing a service as long as there are passengers to be carried.

E Boyes.

ERIC BOYES
Managing Director
Portsmouth City
Transport Limited

INTRODUCTION

October 1986 marked a milestone in public transport in the Portsmouth area. The effects of the 1985 Transport Act removed full municipal control of public transport and Portsmouth City Transport Ltd., a private company wholly owned by the city council, took responsibility for keeping the wheels turning.

Control of public transport has been in the hands of the Corporation since midnight on Monday December 31, 1900. Since then, it has travelled through many peaks and troughs, good times and bad, always trying to give a reasonably-priced reliable service to the people of Portsmouth and, in later years, to the surrounding areas.

Horse-drawn buses horse-drawn trams, electric trams, buses, trolley buses and, finally, the red and white double deckers — all these have travelled the streets of the city. Behind them there were, and are, many people past and present proud to ease passengers on their way.

Many books, papers and booklets have been written giving the details and mechanics of the routes of tramlines, trolley wires and buses over the past 146 years of recorded public transport.

The author is grateful for information from S.E.Harrison's *Tramways of Portsmouth* and *Portsmouth City Transport 1840 - 1977*, by transport enthusiasts A.F. Milton and L.T.A. Bern, which both give great detail on the various aspects of transport in Portsmouth.

I have endeavoured to include the people who have been involved in transport, many for all their working lives. These men and women have been the backbone of public transport. There have been sad times but also many happy and humorous ones. Who would believe that a houseful of furniture could be moved across Portsmouth in the early hours of the morning on a tram? It happened more than once.

I have been involved in public transport for nearly 30 years, working in several local authority departments. There is only one job I have never done and that's punching tickets as a conductor. Bus driving can be enjoyable but very frustrating at times. The last 30 years have been very happy ones: the past eleven years in Portsmouth, the best.

ERIC WATTS

CHAPTER I

BEFORE CORPORATION TRANSPORT

The earliest record of public transport is in 1840 when it is believed that The Portsea Island Conveyance Company ran a horse-bus service between the developing residential areas of North End and Southsea. By 1857 horse-bus services were operating between Old Portsmouth, Portsea, and Landport from Grove Road, Southsea.

The Landport and Southsea Tramways Act of 1863 authorised the company to operate a street tramway with a capital of £10,000 and the first route opened on May 15, 1865, between the South Western Railway station (now Portsmouth and Southsea) and Southsea Pier (Clarence Pier). This provided a transfer service for passengers to the Isle of Wight. At this time, the railway had not been allowed to pass through the defensive walls surrounding Old Portsmouth to the harbour.

Other Acts of Parliament were to follow: the Portsmouth Street Tramways Act of 1870 containing a clause that would allow the local authority to purchase the tramway system; the Portsmouth Street Tramways (Extension Order) 1874; the Landport, Southsea and Portsea Tramways Order 1877; the Portsmouth Tramways Act 1879; the Portsmouth Street Tramways Amalgamation Act 1883; Portsmouth Street Tramways Act 1896; and the Portsmouth Corporation Tramways Act of 1898 which authorised the Corporation to raise the money to purchase the tramway system.

Several operators were running services from the town station to The Hard, Portsea. Priors Omnibuses went between the Bedford Hotel, Commercial Road, and Clarendon Road, Southsea, via the town station and Kings Road. The Conveyance Company omnibuses ran between Southsea and The Hard via the town station.

The Provincial Tramway Company had a feeder service for its horse-drawn trams commencing on March 15, 1878, when its tramway system between the Queen's Hotel and Palmerston Road at Southsea was extended; this service was withdrawn on September 8, 1879. The same company operated a bus service between North End and Cosham from about 1883. Further services were introduced but quickly fell out of use as the tramway was constructed.

The first known motor bus service was operated by Mr. Arthur Julian in 1899 between Clarence Pier and South Parade Pier during the summer. A more regular service ran in 1902 between The Hard and Fratton via Queen Street, Portsea, and Arundel Street, Landport, using two buses named "Cambria" and Albion" but the following year the company went into liquidation.

THE GREAT
TRAMWAY
NUISANCE!!!

FELLOW SUFFERERS,

We have long been subject to this dangerous and crying evil. Some good men and true have at last taken the matter up, and if we support them as we ought,

THE

ODIOUS TRAMWAY
MUST COME UP.

Attend the Meeting on WEDNESDAY EVENING NEXT, at Half-past Seven o'clock, at the LANDPORT HALL, ARUNDEL STREET, and show that you are determined that our principal Highway shall no longer be encroached upon; that life and limb shall not be endangered; that the public traffic shall not be obstructed; and that the livelihood of many a poor working man shall not be taken away for the purpose of filling the pockets of a clique of greedy and monopolising speculators.

A POOR CABBY.

Landport,
14th September, 1867.

TO THE TRADESMEN

OF

Landport & Southsea.

WHAT ARE THE

TRAMWAY COMPANY

DOING FOR US?

1.—They are monopolizing a considerable portion of some of our most important thoroughfares, without payment of rent or compensation!

2.—They are conveying the Passengers to the Isle of Wight, direct from the Railway Station to the Southsea Pier, to the loss and injury of Tradesmen, Cab and Omnibus proprietors and drivers, and everybody else, excepting the Pier and Steam Packet Companies and themselves!

3.—They are causing a most dangerous nuisance—imperilling the safety of persons, horses, and vehicles, and seriously impeding the public traffic!

Shall we silently submit any longer? Let us all unite in getting rid of so crying an evil! No half measures! It is "NOW OR NEVER!"

A TRADESMAN.

Commercial Road, Landport,
September 16th, 1867.

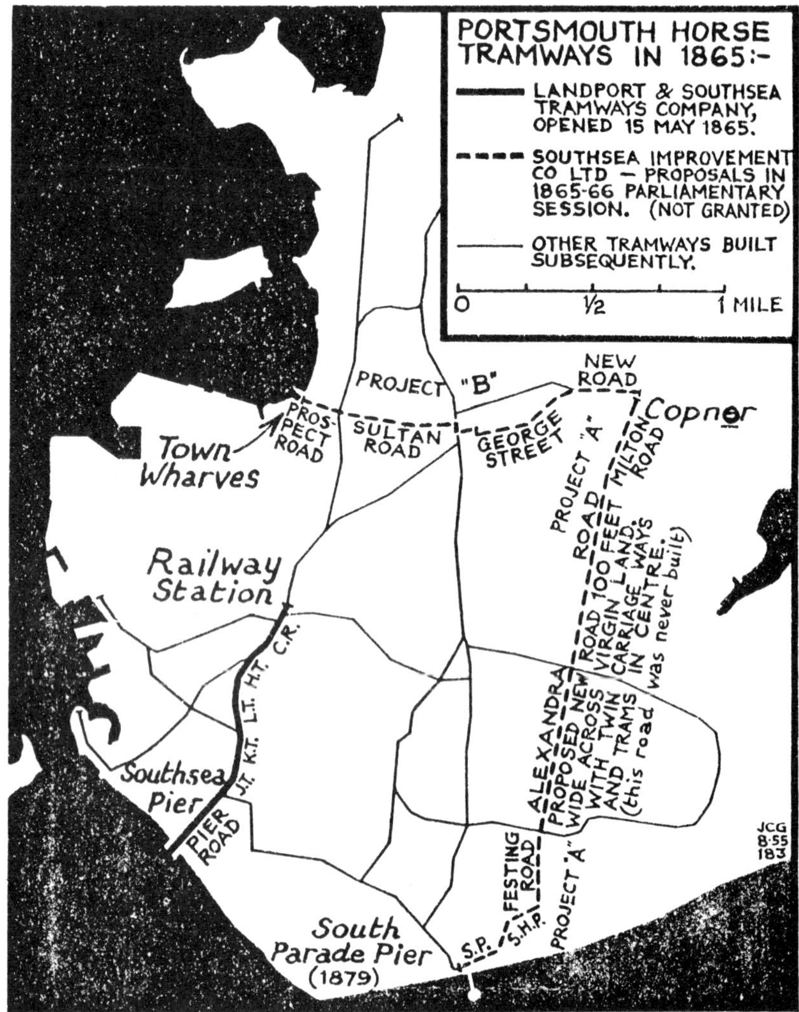

A Provincial horse-drawn tram passes under the railway bridge at Portsmouth and Southsea Station. The road surface under the bridge was lowered on the west side when the tramway was electrified and on the east when trolley buses were introduced.

(T.H. Dethridge)

Typical horse-drawn buses which operated in Portsmouth from 1840 to about 1920. The Provincial Tramway Company used the buses as feeder services for its tramway system but the Corporation did not take them over.

(C.P.P.T.D.)

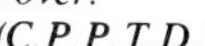

Advertising is much in evidence on this tram at the Clarence Pier, Southsea, terminus. Mumbys, of Gosport, was known for its mineral waters and W. Pink was a small chain of popular grocery shops.

(T.H. Dethridge)

GEORGE F. MILNES & Co.,

(Motor Department), LTD.

"Motoria," Balderton St., Oxford St., LONDON, W.

Works—HADLEY, near WELLINGTON.

MILNES' MOTORS

GOLD MEDAL AND DIPLOMA MERIT, LIVERPOOL TRIALS, FOR LORRY.

GOLD MEDAL, GLASGOW RELIABILITY TRIALS, FOR PLEASURE CARS.

AUTOMOBILE CLUB'S SHOW,

AGRICULTURAL HALL.

Stands 54 and 20. Latest Patterns.

SPECIALITIES:

Public Service Cars. Lorries. Delivery Vans. Sanitary Dust Carts.

DELIVERIES ONE MONTH FROM ORDER.

TELEGRAPHIC ADDRESS—"MILNESIE, LONDON."

One of the first motor buses in Portsmouth, operated by Mr. A. Julian on a route from the Town Hall to Fratton Park. The photograph is reproduced from an advertisement in the Automoto magazine *of April, 1902.*

CHAPTER II

PORTSMOUTH CORPORATION TRAMWAYS

The 1865 tramway between the town station to Clarence Pier is regarded as the first statutory tramway in this country and the Tramways Committee was formed in February, 1896, but it was not until 1898 that the Portsmouth Corporation Tramways Act authorised the council to raise money to purchase the existing tramway system and electrify it. The Portsmouth Street Tramways Act of 1870 had given power to the local authority to purchase the whole of the tramway system operating within the borough from the existing tramway companies.

The Corporation hinted in 1896 that it intended to exercise its right to take over the system from Provincial Tramways Company Limited, which registered in 1872 as the holding company for companies operating tramway systems in several large cities, including Cardiff and Plymouth. The local company, Portsmouth Street Tramways Ltd., had been formed in 1882 from several other smaller companies which had built up a comprehensive tramway system through the various Acts of Parliament.

In May, 1897, the Tramways Committee visited Bristol to see the construction of its electric tramway system. Members were not too impressed; however, after lengthy debates, it was agreed to make the company an offer for the tramway system. On November 22, 1898, the purchase was agreed by the council with a take-over date of midnight on December 31, 1899.

Mr. E. Rotter, who had been working in Edinburgh building cable tramways, was confirmed as the first Engineer and Manager in July, 1899.

Shortly before Christmas 1899, the Tramway Committee decided it did not wish to take over the omnibuses or wedding and funeral carriage owned by the company. The chairman led a deputation to take over formally the assets of the company but the manager had adopted an attitude of "all or nothing". There followed a series of discussions and arguments, finally resolved in court in April 1900 when the judges ruled that the omnibuses etc. were not part of the tramway. On June 14, agreement was reached whereby the company retained the omnibuses but the Corporation was granted running powers over the proposed Portsdown and Horndean Light Railway as far as Portsdown Hill/Widley Lane.

The amount to be paid to the tramway company went to arbitration and the sum was fixed at £185,633. Originally, the company claimed £280,669 after an offer of £205,964 had been made by the Corporation.

At a special committee meeting on January 1, 1901, the chairman reported that the Mayor, himself, the vice-chairman, the Town Clerk and Mr. Rotter formally

PORTSMOUTH TRAMWAYS.

Table of Fares and Distances, October, 1900.

COSHAM TO CLARENCE PIER.

	Yds.	
Through Fare	7,552	4d.
Cosham and Town Hall	6,142	3d.
Hilsea and Clarence Pier	5,759	3d.
Cosham and Kingston Cross	3,784	2d.
Hilsea and Charlotte Street	4,799	2d.
North End and Clarence Pier	4,443	2d.
Cosham and Hilsea	1,993	1d.
Copsey's Siding and Kingston Cross	2,238	1d.
North End and Sultan Road	1,528	1d.
Stamshaw Lane and Railway Station	2,012	1d.
Charlotte Street and Victoria Hall	1,140	1d.
Railway Station and King's Road	841	1d.
Victoria Hall and Clarence Pier	1,267	1d.

COSHAM TO MARMION ROAD.

	Yds.	
Through Fare	7,629	4d.
Cosham and Fratton Station	5,954	3d.
Hilsea and Marmion Road	5,636	3d.
Cosham and Kingston Cross	3,784	2d.
Hilsea and St. Mary's Road	3,065	2d.
North End and Marmion Road	4,320	2d.

had taken over the tramway. The scene was set for progress and expansion of the existing horse-drawn tram system that had been developed during the previous 35 years and for the next 30 years Portsmouth Corporation Tramways proved a highly successful undertaking.

The decision to electrify the existing system was taken following visits by Tramway Committee members to inspect different forms of tramways at Willesden, London, Dover, Paris and Rouen. They recommended the system using overhead power supply.

The probable expenditure for 1901 was put at £347,322 to pay for construction of overhead equipment, permanent way and underground feeders and including work on the existing lines and proposed extensions. A site at Vivash Road, Fratton, behind the Co-op buildings was bought for £900 for the power station. The cost of the building and power station equipment was put at £10,515 and £29,656 respectively.

Dick Kerr and Company of Preston was the principal contractor for the construction of the track and tramcar bodies and electrical equipment. McCartney and McElroy constructed the overhead wires, British Insulated Wire supplied cables

Hilsea Arches, looking north, the only route in and out of Portsmouth. This photograph was presented to the Corporation by the company which erected the overhead power lines for the trams. *(C.P.P.T.D.)*

Permanent way gang laying tramlines in Highland Road, Eastney. The labourers, who had to wield hefty hand tools can be distinguished from the foremen by their headgear. The son of the workman fourth from right supplied the photograph. *(E.W. Houghton)*

and feeder pillars, and Brill and Company was contracted for tramway trucks.

Throughout the southern part of Portsmouth a wide range of civil engineering work started with the fixing of overhead equipment and laying new tramlines creating employment but also considerable disruption to the then traffic flow of horses and carts. While all this work required organisation, the council gave permission for one of the tramway engineers to carry out assistant concert secretary work at the Town Hall "provided that it did not interfere with his duties".

Tenders for the supply of essential items constantly were sought: one for fodder gives a comprehensive list of feed for the horses — beans, 4s6d (22½p) per bushel, bran, 5s (25p) per cwt., new-mown hay, £4.10s (£4.50) per ton. One successful tenderer offered to buy back manure at the rate of 2d per horse per week.

As the department became established, it was necessary to rationalise conditions of employment. Mr. Rotter reported to the tramways committee in December, 1901, the various rates of pay and proposals for adjustments. The Chief Inspector's wage was to be £2.10s (£2.50) a week and the inspectors' rate raised from £1.10s (£1.50) to £2 a week. Mr. Rotter said: "These men give practically the whole of their time to their duties."

Drivers' rates of pay varied, depending on which routes were worked, and hours varied between 63 and 67 each week. Mr. Rotter proposed that they should be paid £1.5s (£1.25) per week during their first year, £1.7s6d (£1.37½) in the second year, and £1.10s (£1.50) after three years' service.

Under the proposals, conductors were to receive an increase also; boys 18 to 21 years old were to be paid £1 a week, over-21, £1.2s (£1.10) in their first year, £1.3s6d (£1.17½) in the second and £1.5s (£1.25) after three years.

A useful source of revenue additional to fares always has been advertising. At that time one company offered £17.10s (£17.50) per tramcar annually to advertise on every tramcar.

The first electric tram carrying passengers was due to run on September 19, 1901, but owing to the funeral on that day of the United States President Mr. McKinley, the inauguration was delayed by five days. On September 24, with due ceremony and lavishly decorated, the first electric tram left North End depot, driven by Mrs. Kimber, wife of the Tramway Committee Chairman.

The *Evening News* of that day devoted a whole page to the Electric Traction Inauguration, with a full description of the system. The article starts: "A new era in the system of locomotion in the main thoroughfares of Portsmouth is to be

The first day of electric tram operation, September 24, 1901, when the wife of the Chairman Mrs. Kimber drove the first tram from North End Depot, Gladys Avenue. (C.P.P.T.D.)

Crowds gather at the junction of Kingston Crescent and Commercial Road, Mile End, to watch the gaily-decorated Tramcar Number 1. In the background is the Air Balloon public house. (C.P.P.T.D.)

Clarence Pier tramway terminus c. 1904. A loop track was installed in 1920 to avoid congestion in the popular resort area.

inaugurated today by the opening of the electric tramways for the public service. The event has been long anticipated and we feel sure that the enterprise and spirit which prompted the Corporation to embark upon such a huge undertaking will be fully justified by the results."

It goes on to include thanks to Mr. White for his enterprise, with the Provincial Tramways Company, in extending its system of horse-car trams to nearly all parts of the borough. "On being taken over by the Corporation, however, it was decided not only to reconstruct the existing lines but also to give the inhabitants of the populous districts of Fratton, Kingston and Eastney opportunities for more expeditiously reaching the centre of the town or Dockyard where so many of the working men find employment."

Details are given of the extensions to the system, who did the work, material involved and a graphic description of the current generation, using Babcock and Wilcox patent water tube steam boilers having a total heating surface of 3,580 square feet. These boilers produced steam to drive two engines which each had a 25-ton fly-wheel directly coupled to a continuous current generator and could develop up to 900 indicated horse power. A third engine was slightly smaller.

The new equipment, including the tramcars, required modern facilities. The depot at Gladys Avenue, North End, had been used by the Provincial Company since the early 1880s but extensive alterations were needed to house some 113 trams, with maintenance facilities, pits in the main parking area, a large paintshop with access from a special line and a traversing machine.

It was described in the *Evening News*: "The new car shed will be a large and substantially brick-built edifice with a slate roof supported by light ironwork." On June 27, 1901, the Tramways Committee accepted a quotation from a local builder, J. and M. Patrick, to construct the whole in ten months for £17,780. Office and recreational accommodation for staff was provided over the next three years.

Up to the day the depot closed, November 1, 1981, there was a pair of stable doors at the entrance to what the author knew as the Stores. All that remains of the depot is the rear wall providing a boundary for the small housing estate which covers the site.

Towards the end of 1901, the Tramways Committee was informed that the Portsdown and Horndean Light Railway had appointed Mr. Rotter as its Engineer. Mr. Rotter was retained as a consultant to the Corporation until the proposed work was completed.

In March, 1902, Mr. W.R. Spaven, who had worked for Leeds City Transport as Traffic Manager, was appointed General Manager, and Mr. V. Lironi, whose experience in electric motive power was considerable, was appointed Engineer.

Mr. Lironi had worked for the Electrical Locomotive and Power Company and run the cars of the first electrical locomotive; his expertise was to prove invaluable. Among his innovations was the conversion of the boilers at Vivash Road Power Station to run on oil instead of coal during the Miners Strike of 1921 — a facility retained until the closure of the power station.

Mr. Spaven was appointed on a salary of £300 a year, rising by £25 annually to £350. Mr. Lironi's starting salary was £200 a year, and the Transport Committee decreed that he should "devote the whole of his time to the service of the Corporation".

With the extensions and improvements at North End depot complete, it was decided to lease the former tram depot at Broad Street, Old Portsmouth, to Portsmouth and Gosport Motors for seven years at £65 a year. Capstan House now stands on the site.

Incentives for passengers were introduced: ten one penny tickets could be bought for 9d (4p) but were not valid for workmen's journeys. And to encourage safety, from March 31, 1903, at the discretion of the General Manager, drivers were paid a bonus of 10s (50p) if they drove for six months free from accident.

At a meeting of the Traffic Sub-Committee on January 20, 1903, the following fares were recommended:

	1903	1986
Main Line Hilsea (Coach and Horses) to Kingston Cres.	1d	34p
Hilsea to Town Hall	2d	38p
Hilsea to Clarence Pier	3d	40p
Fratton Line North End to South Parade Pier	2d	38p
Hilsea to South Parade Pier	3d	44p
Circular Route Palmerston Road and Charlotte Street	1d	34p
Fratton Bridge and Charlotte Street	2d	32p
Copnor and Dockyard Route Copnor and Dockyard	2d	34p
Eastney and Floating Bridge Eastney and Bradford Road	1d	32p
Dockyard and South Parade Pier Route Dockyard and Palmerston Road	1d	34p
Dockyard and South Parade Pier	2d	34p

These were to be implemented from March 31, 1903. The stages noted are only those that can be compared with similar ones, for 1986.

In spite of the last horse-drawn tramcar having run in May, 1903, tenders for fodder were still being sought in May, 1905. Probably the horses were used for maintenance workers' transport. Photographs of laying the tramlines in Twyford Avenue, Stamshaw show horses and carts and the City Museum has a horse-drawn tower wagon waiting for a permanent home.

A woman conductor waits by the entrance to her tram at Cosham tramway terminus about 1920. A tram ride to go to the Portsdown Hill fair was a special event for many Portsmouth people. The passenger shelter in the background was made from the body of a horse-drawn tram. *(C. Phillips)*

Tramcar Number 80 was decorated overall to mark the visit of the German fleet to Portsmouth in 1907. The photograph was taken in North End depot by tram driver J.L. Seekings who recorded many special events and scenes of accidents for the Department. (C.P.P.T.D.)

Laying tramlines along Goldsmith Avenue for the Milton extension in about 1909. The bridge in the background was over the branch line to Southsea which was closed in the early-1920s. (C.P.P.T.D.)

A more-detailed view of the Milton extension looking east in about 1909. The Shepherd's Crook public house is in the background on its original site where the gates to Milton Park are now. (C.P.P.T.D.)

By now, a comprehensive list of rules and regulations for motormen and conductors had been introduced, requiring all employees to be honest, punctual, obedient, sober, civil and alert.

On the occasion of the visit of the French fleet during the late summer of 1905, five special cars were decorated and a further 78 decorated to a design submitted by Fred Wilkins and Bros. Ltd. for a cost of £108. All tram standards from the Dockyard to North End were decorated at a cost of 8s9d (43p) each, plus a supply of various flags.

In August 1905, Mr. Spaven reported an operating surplus for the year ending March 31, of £13,530, which was transferred to the Reserve Fund.

From 1902 to 1913, the system continued to develop to a total of 34 route miles.

In 1906, Vivash Road power station was extended and there were attempts to increase routes further but these were considered a reckless and unnecessary expenditure. In spite of this reservation, by 1909, the Milton extension was built.

With the completion of the electrification of the whole of the network, the increase in traffic highlighted various problems, one of which was Portsbridge. For military security, the bridge had a swing span but, although permission had been obtained to put a cable across the bridge, it had to be strengthened as a fixed structure at a cost of £250 to £300. Tramcars then had to take the precaution of travelling over the bridge at 2 - 4 miles per hour.

Tenders for further work to complete North End depot with workshops and offices were approved and carried out at a cost of £8,150.

Owing to the success of the system and the need for more rolling stock, it was decided to convert four horse-drawn tramcars to electric power. Cars number 81 to 84 were converted in the department's workshop. Their principal use throughout their life was on special journeys on bank holidays and for staff transport between depots and the Town Hall to 1936.

Car 84 is preserved at Eastney depot after 40 years' storage at North End. The move was made in the winter of 1976, following part of the original route via Fratton Bridge and Albert Road.

In April 1903, the Town Council considered a proposal by the Hayling Light Railway Tramway for a service using a conveyor bridge across Langstone Harbour to an area near the pumping station at Henderson Road, Eastney. The plan was approved, subject to stringent conditions, but it never happened.

With the completion of the electrification programme and with North End depot workshops operational, it was decided to lease to Curtis and Sons the former tram depot at The Hard, Portsea, for 21 years at £75 a year. The site is now occupied by the former signal box at the entrance to Portsmouth Harbour station.

A water car for cleaning the rails, fleet number 101, was bought for £655 from Dick Kerr and Co. In later years, citizens of Portsmouth were to complain about its use during the night when the rails were ground with carborundum blocks.

In August 1903, Mr. Rotter presented a final report to the Tramways Committee for works and equipment totalling £373,912, including £218,544 for permanent way and feeders, and £49,270 for electric cars.

Considering the amount of work involved, the relatively short time taken and the lack of modern technology and equipment, Mr. Rotter's efforts in carrying out the major project were commendable. Such a scheme today would still be considered a major development and could be estimated at about £14,500,000.

Mr. Rotter's service as Consultant Engineer was ended and reported to the Tramways Committee of February, 1904. He then continued working for the Portsdown and Horndean Light Railway.

Mr. Lironi reported that he was experiencing problems with tram tyres which were operating for only 12,000 miles instead of the expected 23,000 miles, and

Two Portsmouth businesses which no longer existed by the 1980s are advertised on the side of tramcar Number 37 which is waiting at Cosham terminus before travelling on a route through North End to Palmerston Road in about 1930. *(R.C. Riley)*

***Built in 1880 as a horse-drawn tram,** tramcar Number 84 was converted to electric traction in 1903 and remained in service until 1936. Its last repaint was in 1960 for the 50th anniversary of the Department. It was stored at North End depot until 1976 and is now at Eastney although it is owned by Portsmouth City Museums.*

the department was running an additional five cars. Permission was given for 150 tyres to equip 80 tramcars to be ordered from Hadfields of Sheffield at a cost of £3.7s6d (£3.37½). The metal tyres were fitted by heating them in a hearth and shrinking on to the original wheel.

In May 1904, the formation of a figure-eight principal route on the Inner Circle Route was agreed because of the increase in the number of passengers. At the same meeting the Tramways Committee approved the drawing of the first cheque for £45 for paying accident-free bonuses to 90 motormen.

Coal was being purchased for the power station on a regular basis and a tender from Bradway and Son Co. Ltd. shows best Welsh smokeless coal could be bought at 20s11d (£1.10) a ton.

Further expenditure was approved for a crossover and overhead equipment near the Beach Mansion Hotel (now the Hospitality Inn) near South Parade Pier, Southsea, to provide siding accommodation at a total cost of about £200. Later, a full loop was installed.

Tenders for plates to be used at tram stops were sought from supplies. The familiar signs "All cars stop here by request" cost 6s (30p) and were expected to last ten years — many lasted much longer.

In January, 1905, the department paid £63 to the Inland Revenue for licences on 84 tramcars.

The full list of services was:

A	Cosham, North End, Commercial Road, Town Hall, The Terraces, Clarence Pier.
B	Twyford Avenue, Commercial Road, Town Hall, Blackfriars Road, Albert Road, South Parade Pier, The Circle, Victoria Road, Fratton Road, North End, Cosham (in this direction only).
X	Cosham to Twyford Avenue (reverse of B).
C	Dockyard, Alexandra Road, Osborne Road, South Parade Pier, Festing Road, Eastney, Milton, Goldsmith Avenue, Blackfriars Road, Town Hall (extended to Dockyard or Clarence Pier as required).
D	Copnor Bridge, Lake Road, Town Hall, The Terraces, Clarence Pier (Sundays and bank holidays only, weather permitting).
Former E	North End, Fratton Road, Fawcett Road, Waverley Road, Osborne Road, The Terraces, Town Hall, Commercial Road, North End (circular route in both directions, weekdays only).
G	Dockyard, Park Road, Town Hall, Blackfriars Road, Fawcett Road, Waverley Road, South Parade Pier.
H	Fratton Bridge, Victoria Road, Osborne Road, Clarence Pier.
J	Copnor Bridge, Lake Road, Town Hall, High Street, Floating Bridge.
L	Floating Bridge, High Street, Town Hall, Blackfriars Road, Albert Road, Eastney, Milton, Goldsmith Avenue, Blackfriars Road, Town Hall (in this direction only, extended to Clarence Pier as required).
Z	Town Hall to Floating Bridge (reverse of L).
M	Eastney, Albert Road, Victoria Road, Fratton Road, North End, Cosham (Sundays and bank holidays only, weather permitting).

On Sundays and bank holidays only, in lieu of "circular route", these two services were worked without route letters: Cosham (or North End) via Commercial Road and Town Hall to Clarence Pier; Cosham (or North End) via Fratton Road and Fawcett Road to South Parade Pier.

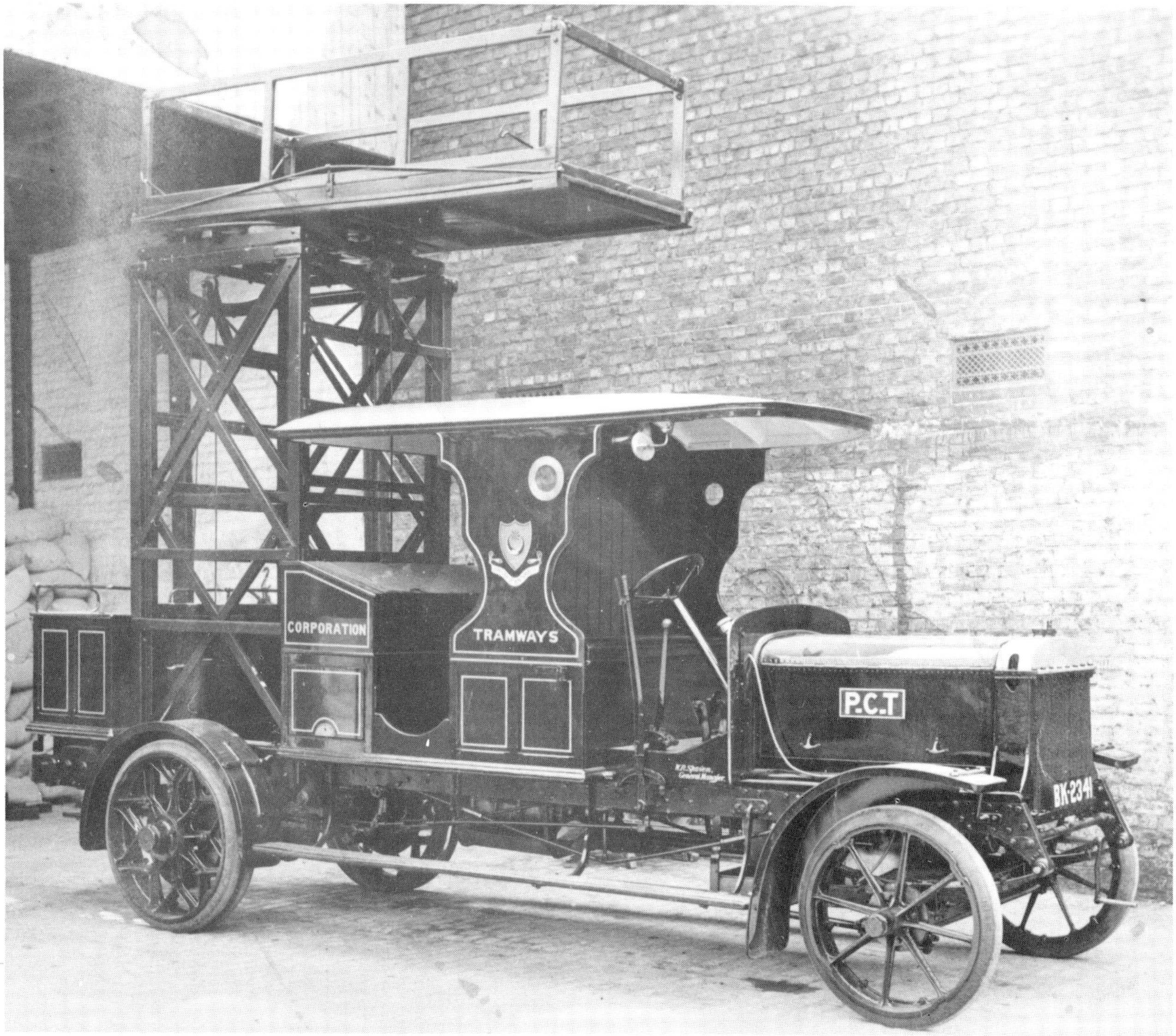

The first motorised tower wagon, pictured in 1914 was used for the maintenance of overhead cables. (E.W. Houghton)

Coal to fuel the Vivash Road power station was transported from the nearby Fratton Goods Yard in an A.E.C. lorry in about 1914. (E.W. Houghton)

The laying of interlacing track for the extension to Alexandra Park from Rudmore attracted a lot of onlookers in about 1923. The Tramway Department was responsible for the maintenance of the roadway at either side and between the tram tracks. *(C.P.P.T.D.)*

Horse-drawn carts were used to remove debris as the surface of Twyford Avenue, Stamshaw, was prepared for tramlines. All the men were employed by the Tramway Department on a temporary basis. *(C.P.P.T.D.)*

Another cause for celebration was the inauguration of the Festing Road tramway from Highland Road, in July, 1913, enabling people to reach the attractions of Canoe Lake by tram. *(C.P.P.T.D.)*

From July 4, 1913, trams ran to Alexandra Park along Twyford Avenue. The links between South Parade Pier and Albert Road were opened 27 days later and the section of road between the White House, Milton, and the Highland Chief at Eastney, were connected on September 22.

Wartime saw a reduction in the tramway services as many motormen and conductors were with the armed forces and businessmen and women volunteers were trained to drive and conduct trams. The office diary records that the first conductresses were engaged on July 4, 1915. In November, a Mrs. Tilly and a Mrs. Chiverton were appointed as supervisors. The bonus granted to the men was passed on to the women but it was some years before they enjoyed equal pay.

In June, 1914, route letters to distinguish the services, which previously had been used for administrative purposes only, were displayed on the tramcars.

At the end of the financial year March 1917, £14,000 was used for the relief of rates and the renewals fund stood at £72,088, with a net surplus of £18,680.

As early as 1907, the Tramway Committee had considered obtaining permission to run motor buses but deferred its decision, no doubt due to the vehicles' unreliability and poor suspension. Again, in 1911, the council considered motor bus operation and deferred a decision. It seems likely that there was some public outcry about the "old bone shaker" omnibuses operated by private companies running over indifferent roads; the trams had been described as a smooth and silent ride.

In May, 1919, a "toast rack car" was brought from Southampton for £550. It was given the fleet number 104 and was the only "toast rack car" operated by the Corporation. Built to resemble a boat, it was decorated for Christmas 1933 and several other special occasions.

In his report to the council dated December 16, 1918, Mr. Spaven expressed his concern over the ability to cope with increases in traffic. The statistical returns show an increase of 14,000,000 over the pre-war year of 1914.

To deal with this situation, he had 100 cars, of which 92 operated a daily service, leaving only eight for maintenance.

It was resolved that the permanent way should be put in a satisfactory condition and the General Manager was given permission to employ the appropriate staff. The repairs to the tracks were to cause many problems for the department in later years.

A proposal was made for 25 new double-deck cars to be bought and six of the older cars converted to "toast racks". However, 12 cars eventually were bought and no conversions made.

Authorisation to extend the tramway system from the junction of Milton Road/Goldsmith Avenue along Milton Road and Copnor Road to the existing line in London Road at Hilsea was given by the Tramway Committee but the work was never carried out.

At its March, 1919, meeting, the committee agreed that an order be placed for ten Thornycroft 40 h.p. War Office J-type buses with lowered radiator chassis, complete with Wadham bodies made at Waterlooville at a cost of £1,274, each complete with bodies painted and ready for use on the road.

A B.A.V. lighting set and water pump in lieu of the thermo syphon system was considered an extra. Six were to be delivered in July 1919 and four the following month. Some were used for relief services during the peace celebrations.

An open "toast rack" tram, so called because of the arrangement of its seats, pictured in North End depot. It was bought in 1919 from Southampton Corporation. *(C.P.P.T.D.)*

By 1932, the same tram afforded a little more protection for its passengers by the addition of a canopy. *(C.P.P.T.D.)*

Full of happy children and their parents, a toast rack tram was decorated with illuminations for Children's Joy Week in 1933. (C.P.P.T.D.)

Crowds gathered in London Road, North End, to see the toast rack tramcar decorated for George V's silver jubilee. Daytime photographs of the dressed trams in use are rare. (L. Bern)

In the 1930s there was a lot of interest in the pioneers of aviation and the Schneider Trophy races, held over the Solent, attracted many spectators. The toast rack tram has the motto "Progress in the Air". (P. Couper)

Tramcar Number 80 was decorated to take part in the victory celebratons for the end of the First World War in 1919. Sir John Timpson, wearing his Mayoral chain, is standing at the steps with the General Manager, Mr. W. Spaven, at the controls. (H. Draper)

'The Spare Hand Sheet

Working conditions for the early Corporation employees were very poor — no Health and Safety at Work Act or Employment Protection Act. All new starters had to learn the job in their own time; they were then put on "The Spare Hand Sheet", a term still used today but under very different conditions. The Spare Hand was told to report for duty when there might be work for him. If there was a spare duty due to sickness or oversleeping by the regular hand, then he would be paid, otherwise it was no work, no pay.

Carelessness costs

Discipline was quite harsh but some of the tram operators were negligent at times. George Frederick Bawley, who started working for the Provincial Tramway Company in March, 1900, did not have a very good record. In July 1901, he was cautioned for allowing a passenger to have a 2d ride for 1d. In November, he broke a dashlight glass that cost him a shilling (5p) for the repair. On Christmas Eve, 1901, he received a day's suspension for moving the trolley pole before passengers had got off the tram. When Inspector Randall spoke to him about it, he was insolent. For neglecting to take a fare, he was cautioned in June, 1902. The end finally came in September, 1902. The record book reads: "Inspector Ade saw a lady give this conductor something which he thought was her fare but he did not give a ticket. When spoken to, he said she had given him a penny for himself. The Inspector caught up to her and she stated that she got on at Fratton Bridge and paid the Conductor as she was leaving the car. His excuse was on the return journey that he dropped a penny in giving change and did not stop to look for it, he thought the lady had picked it up." The column headed Verdict shows: Dismissed 1/10/02.

The truck of tramcar Number 59 was built by Brill and its equipment was by Dick Kerr. It started operating in 1901 and ran until 1935. After refurbishing in 1925 it was equipped with curtains and a comprehensive destination board. Known to some as meny boards.
(C. Phillips)

Cautionary tales

There are numerous reports in the discipline book when one-day suspensions were given for failing to collect fares. Arriving for duty a few minutes late guaranteed a cautioning note.

Harry Allen started his employment in August, 1901, and, still new to the job, on September 13, he received a day's suspension for leaving his cash bag in the Harness Room, Fratton, instead of placing it in the cash box. He received a caution in January, 1902, for neglecting to look out for passengers; by September, he resigned.

There was no such thing as industrial accidents. William Somerset Cross who started as a conductor in March, 1902, was unfortunate enough to accidentally break a window. He was going to his box under the stairs when the tram went round a corner too fast, he lost his balance and his elbow went through a window. He was cautioned and had to pay half a crown (12½p), being half the cost of the damage.

Joke was on conductor

Mr. Reg Webber, a ticket machine mechanic at Highland Road offices, tells of an experience of his father, Driver W.W. Webber, when picking up passengers in Palmerston Road. "Do you take farthings?", one intending lady passenger asked his conductor. Being a jovial sort of chap, he replied: ."Yes, madam, we take anything — bottles, jamjars, donkey stones, rags and bones, anything." Unfortunately, the lady saw fit to report the jolly conductor and he was soon "down the road" with his cards in his hands.

Driver Webber himself was in trouble before the town magistrates, charged under a public health Act for driving his tramcar to the common danger. After 17 years of driving trams, he was found guilty and fined £1 for hitting a horse-drawn dray, causing it to swing round so tht a packing case fell off and broke one of the tramcar's windows. Although he was "admonished", he was not sacked.

He was told on another occasion to decide where his loyalties lay after he and three fellow motormen, shooting for his local public house, had beaten the Tramway rifle team. Due to his nine years' military service, most of it in India, Driver Webber was a good shot. His misplaced loyalty in shooting for the pub rather than the Tramways earned him and his mates an ultimatum from their boss: "If you want to continue working for us, then you had better shoot for the Tramway team."

CHAPTER III

THE FIRST MOTOR BUSES

Ironically, the first motor buses were bodied by Wadhams, now Wadham Stringer (Coachbuilders), of Waterlooville, and the last single-deckers delivered to the Corporation were Dennis Lancet chassis with a Wadham Stringer body, delivered in February, 1982.

The first motor bus route started on August 11, 1919, operating between Devonshire Avenue, the Dockyard, Arundel Street and St. Mary's Road. These buses were given the fleet numbers 1 - 10. Number 10, still owned by the department, has since been re-numbered 1 and is stored at Eastney depot. It sometimes goes out on special occasions to rallies and promotional exercises as far afield as Le Havre.

After about six years' service, problems developed with the bodies, no doubt due to the condition of the roads, solid rubber tyres and very hard suspension. The original Wadham bodies were replaced with secondhand bodies from the London General Omnibus Company at a cost of £25 each, the work being carried out by the department's own staff.

Cosham terminus was opened on February 27, 1920, on an area now taken up by the bowling green and tennis courts and extending to the railway line.

One of the last buses bought by the Department was bus Number 97, which has a body by Wadham Stringers, of Waterlooville; on a Dennis Lancet chassis. *(G.H. Truran)*

One of the first motor buses bought by the Department, bus Number 10, had a Thornycroft chassis and body by Wadham Brothers, of Waterlooville. It was renumbered Number 1 in 1942. fitted with an ex-L.G.O.C. body in 1927. The bus is now owned by Portsmouth Museums and stored at Eastney depot. *(C.H.T. Marshall)*

Six of the first ten motor buses bought by Portsmouth Corporation, pictured outside the former Heroes of Waterloo public house in July, 1919. The bodies, by Wadham Brothers, of Waterlooville, were on Thornycroft chassis. *(C.H.T. Marshall)*

A rear view of the Thornycroft BK 2986 showing its tightly-curving stairs to the top deck. *(C.P.P.T.D.)*

This path marks the line of tramway from the Portsea Island boundary to Cosham compound. The poplar trees were planted in 1930 when the junction of the Portsmouth Corporation system and the Portsdown and Horndean Light Railway was relaid opposite the Portsbridge Hotel, Cosham.

The borough boundary, from October 1, 1920, extended to the New Inn, Drayton, in the east, Paulsgrove House in the west and to the Boundary Oak just over the top of Portsdown Hill past the George Inn to the north. Since 1903, the Corporation had a right under its inter-running agreement with the Portsdown and Horndean Light Railway to run trams to Portsdown Hill. It is understood some 6,000 trips were made carrying no passengers, but a day trip to the Hill on bank holidays was a popular event for residents of Portsmouth.

With the boundaries extended beyond the top of the Hill, the Corporation ran buses on Wednesdays, Saturdays and Sundays, using the Thorneycrofts.

On August 1, 1924, a through service of Light railway cars was started between Horndean and Portsmouth Town Hall at a fare of 9d (4p) and from December 15, the service was extended to Palmerston Road, Southsea. In the 1925 season it ran to Clarence Pier on Sundays and bank holidays. Finally, from April, 1927, it was extended from Palmerston Road to South Parade Pier on a daily basis. Passengers were issued with two tickets — a company ticket when travelling north of Cosham and a Corporation ticket for the southern part of the journey.

Between October 5, 1920, and November 11, 1920, 12 double-deck top-covered car bodies were delivered and given fleet numbers 105 — 116. They were delivered in sections to Cosham railway station, the bodies taken by lorry to North End depot and the chassis pulled along the tram track. The trams, each costing £1,930, were then assembled in the workshops. This purchase was part of Mr. Spaven's plan to increase the fleet size and improve the quality of the rolling stock; they were to give valuable service for many years.

By 1920, work was under way on numerous repairs to the original tramway tracks as many lines had become badly worn. Major work relaying tramlines was to continue into the 1930s, causing problems for other road users and passengers.

In November, 1922, the Tramways Committee applied to the Board of Trade for a loan of £193,000 for the repairs. Three Foden steam wagons for carrying the equipment and materials were bought with a stone-crushing machine. The wagons had a power take-off arrangement providing power to drive the stone-crushing machine but it was not very successful in its task of crushing the setts removed from the roadway for use as ballast. Two of the steam wagons were later sold to the City Engineer's Department for £100 each. The third stayed with the tramways until about 1932. One of its final jobs was to move furniture and equipment from Vivash Road to the Highland Road offices.

From the early days Vivash Road power station had played an important part in the tramway system, providing power from the day the first electric tram ran. In March, 1926, a new generating plant was opened by Portsmouth Corporation Electricity Department and the Vivash Road site converted to a bus depot where the Thorneycrofts were kept. It also housed a drawing table 33 feet long used for drawing detailed plans of the tramway system. In addition to its own plans, the department held plans for the Portsdown Light Railway and the Gosport system.

Vivash Road was vacated in March, 1932, following the opening of the depot and offices at Highland Road. By July, 1933, the entire buildings were sold under the auctioneer's hammer for £6,750. All that remains today of the power station is a wall of white glazed bricks, which were part of the main building, at the rear of the Co-op store in Fratton Road.

The wall with white glazed bricks is all that remains of Vivash Road Power Station. It, too, is threatened with the redevelopment of the neighbouring Co-op store in Fratton Road.

In the 1920s,post-war depression had settled over the country; times were hard and businesses fluctuated according to the prosperity of the town.

Towards the end of the First World War, a national transport workers federation, forerunner of today's Transport and General Workers Union, was formed. In 1923, the men of the department formed their own benevolent society which provided relief for workmates who fell on hard times.

An office diary gives an indication of what was happening: for example, from the week ending November 8, 1921. there were reductions in pay of 2s (10p) for employees over 18 and 1s (5p) for those under-18, representing pay cuts of about five per cent. on wages of £2 a week.

Other measures were taken to save money, similar to those that have been used throughout the history of the department, such as adjusting the frequency of service. There were many occasions when a service started later in the morning, finished earlier at night and 10-minute frequencies were decreased to 15 minutes over periods of several weeks.

A musicians' strike which closed Portsmouth's many theatres from November 21 to December 4, 1921, was noted in the diary. No doubt the lack of private cars made trams and buses the only means of transport to and from evening entertainment for ordinary folk. Tramways men were on short time working of a five-day week and a 15-minute service all day.

The wage rates and earning potential for the men varied considerably. Full-time working was reintroduced a week later and the 10-minute frequency resumed. By January 4, 1922, short time working and the 15-minute frequency were back. Then

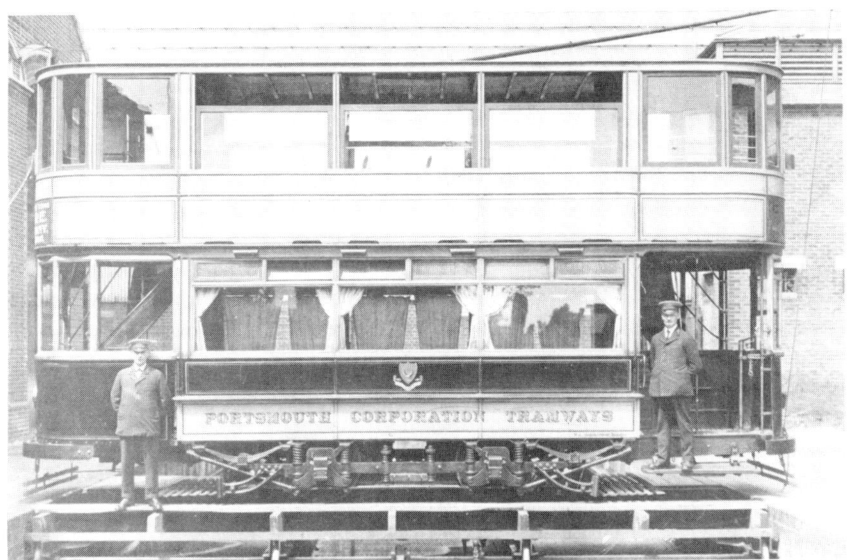

The refined lines of a closed-top tramcar on the traversing machine at North End depot, in about 1920. (C.P.P.T.D.)

Highland-Road head office was built in 1932. The imposing frontage of the building is now the subject of a preservation order. *(C.P.P.T.D.)*

The brick and stone front of the office was decorated with bunting for the Coronation of George VI. *(C. Phillips)*

in February there was a further wage reduction of 3s (15p) a week for men and 1s6d (7p) for under-18s.

Up to 1931/2, considerable reconstruction of the tramway was carried out, leading to many diversions. A diary entry for November 3, 1922, records: During the reconstruction of track in Osborne Road, the C route cars will travel between the Dockyard and Queens Hotel and between Osborne Road and South Parade Pier the C. route service will terminate at Queens Hotel on the one side and near Palmerston Road on the other side." One must assume that through passengers walked between the two points. Other areas where track reconstruction took place included between North End and Hilsea, Arundel Street, Greetham Street, and between Rudmore and Alexandra Park, where the service was maintained by buses.

Still, experimental work was carried out on new types of point controllers in various sections of the tramway. Normally, the points were operated by youngsters known as Point Boys who were employed straight from school. If they were lucky enough, they were taken on as conductors and gradually climbed the ladder of success. One Point Boy known to the author was promoted successively to conductor, driver, inspector, chief inspector and, finally, traffic officer — the most senior position in the traffic department.

In December 1923, a sick pay scheme was introduced for weekly-paid employees under which they would receive half-pay for one month, less half of their National Insurance. In April 1924, a superannuation scheme came into operation but many staff had to wait several years before they were committed to the scheme, some joining only two years before they retired, and there was a long waiting list for a number of years.

From 1920 until the start of the Second World War, many arguments were made public as the department tried to penetrate new areas. The districts beyond Cosham railway gates were well served by the newly-formed Southdown Company and many residents proclaimed the Southdown vehicles were more comfortable, cleaner, and that their drivers were more polite.

The service to Drayton and Farlington was "on and off" for many years until the Regional Traffic Commissioner, during the Second World War, told the company and the Corporation to resolve their problems or he would make an independent judgement. Eventually, a co-ordination agreement was reached in 1946.

Mr. Spaven retired on August 31, 1926, handing over the job of General Manager and Engineer to Mr. Ben Hall, of Halifax, who was appointed at a salary of £1,000 a year from June 26, 1926.

Mr. Hall started at a difficult time; the trams had been running for almost 25 years, giving an excellent service and creating opportunities for the people of Portsmouth to travel cheaply and quickly — but standards were changing rapidly. The travelling public demanded comfort and the general preference was to abandon the trams and introduce the buses.

Comparisons between trams and buses were made on a regular basis and published weekly in the *Evening News*.

In 1920 the trams carried 46 million passengers with a car mileage of 2.9 million, by 1925 this dropped to 39 million passengers with 3.2 million miles.

Weekly figures for July 1931 compared with the previous year:

	1930	1931
Tram receipts	£4,490	£4,313
Bus receipts	£3,473	£4,125
Total passengers	1,368,424	1,426,441
Total mileage	134,749	131,540
Trams in service	84	77
Buses in service	57	55

Mr. F. Prescott, who replaced Mr. Mumford as Traffic Superintendent in February, 1924, was to play an ever-increasing role in organising all the diversions in the town. In addition to supervising the traffic section, he was a keen sportsman, taking an active interest in the football team. He was responsible for introducing several "capped" players from the Transport team to Portsmouth Football Club.

One of his first tasks was to reorganise services to cope with diversions during the demolition of the Goldsmith Avenue railway bridge in July, 1924, and the Jessie Road bridge in February, 1925. Among further problems to be dealt with was the reconstruction of Portsbridge at a time when there was no alternative route out of the town.

During the General Strike of May, 1926, some 100 men stopped work, a relatively small proportion of the employees.

With a bus fleet of 40 various vehicles, it was decided to enter into a contract with Dunlop tyres from January 1, 1927; the contract was changed to Michelin in 1928. Even now, the department does not own a single tyre on a bus — a mileage contract is made with a tyre company, paying a fixed rate for every 1,000 miles operated. Since 1939, the Goodyear Tyre Company has held the contract, having gained the business with a quotation of 0.175d per vehicle mile for petrol and oil-powered vehicles and 0.185d per mile for trolley vehicles, subject to a 3.75 per cent. discount if paid within 37 days. From August, 1940, to April, 1942, there were price increases varying from 17 per cent. to 32 per cent. In September, 1942, a new agreement, on which the present operation is based, was signed.

Tramway deaths

The office diary records many unfortunate incidents, for example on July 21, 1921: "Fatal accident to a soldier E.A.Britnell, R.F.A. at Hilsea. On August 13, 1922, C.P.G. Block, knocked down by car (tramcar) in Kingston Road, injuries proving fatal: — Verdict, Accidental Death."
On December 1, 1923, a Mr. Hall, of Regent Street, jumped off a tram while it was still moving and sustained a fractured skull. The diary notes that he "succumbed" to his injury. The inquest verdict was Accidental death and the conductor was exonerated from blame.

Unfriendly act

Mr. Ray Rolfe tells of a conductor trying to be friendly towards a rather large, matronly lady one morning: "Good morning, my pretty maiden, where are you going this fine morning?" he asked. "I'm going straight to the Guildhall to report you for being too cheeky," she replied. Unfortunately, the conductor received a severe reprimand.

End of the line

There were several instances when trams failed to stop at the Floating Bridge in Old Portsmouth and had to be pulled out of the water. The marks of the rails in the stone setts still can be seen by the old slipway. One incident was due to a conductor trying his hand as a driver — he was taught how to start the tram but not how to stop it.

A points boy, proudly posing in his uniform in 1917, was one of many who were able to progress through a career with the Department from humble beginnings to become a bus driver. *(A. Moody)*

Problems surface

A company called Frank Bevis Ltd. was engaged to move a heavy platform crane from Clarence Pier to a yard in Mile End Road, presumably for repair, using a Foden steam wagon with flanged wheels. The wagon had to travel in front of the Town Hall across the ashphalt roadway, causing damage to the tramway tracks and road surface. The Tramway Department sought compensation from the company, as it was responsible for the upkeep of the tram track, the roadway between the lines and a portion of the roadway at the side of the tracks. In several instances with double track, the department was responsible for the upkeep of the whole width of the roadway and paid rates for the track. In later years this was to become a considerable financial burden.

Pointing the way

Point boys had a hard life. They started at 14 years old, from school, for 25 shillings (£1.25) for seven days a week. Sunday was considered a half day when the trams started at 1 p.m. Christmas Day was the only holiday until the early 1920s when the work was reduced to six days a week but their pay was cut to 17s4d (87p).

The point boy's tool was a long iron bar with a chisel end for insertion into the points mechanism and the other end had a forged ring for handling. Tram drivers carried a points pole made of ash with a forged metal chisel end, one of which is kept at Highland Road depot. Drivers were able to switch the points from their driving position while on the move but if they missed, the tram went the wrong way.

A point boy could have as many as four sets of points to look after, such as at Bradford Junction, Southsea, where three main lines joined. During diversions for reconstruction, the boys were particularly busy as when Commercial Road services were diverted through Kingston and Lake roads. The trams were never more than 15 minutes apart and there were times when some 20 trams passed one point every ten minutes. The tram lines were interlacing track with the occasional loop and points were spring-loaded, requiring setting in one direction only. To prevent trams travelling in the opposite direction on a single track, there was a system of signalling using flags during the day and a hurricane lamp at night until about 1922 when an electric system was introduced. A common occurrence during the winters was smog and then the boys had to guide trams across busy junctions literally by walking in front of them with a lamp.

CHAPTER IV

COMPETITION

For many years, there had been would-be independent operators in Portsmouth. One of the first had attempted to run buses around Portsea but without success; another, a Mr.Outrim, ran a bus in Copnor Road but gave up after a short time in 1925 and became an employee of the Corporation.

The Southsea Tourist Company started business in 1919, running a service within the borough; by the time the Southdown Company took it over in 1925, it operated regular services to Horndean and the Meon Valley. It established a foothold in the town with a service from Clarence Pier via the seafront, Eastney, Milton, and Stubbington Avenue to North End.

Another short-lived company was Portsmouth and District Motor Services Ltd., which started in the early Twenties with a former General Omnibus Company B-type double-decker, similar to the Thornycroft. This company tried a service between Eastney and Cosham but, at that time, the area along Copnor Road was not fully developed and the service did not pay.

In 1923 a company known as Denmead Queen started operations to Denmead and Hambledon and about the same period Blue Motor Services ran to Wickham and Boarhunt. Southdown eventually took over these two companies. By late 1925/early 1926, Southdown had a significant presence in the borough, with services to and from outlying villages.

The origin of Southdown Motor Services is connected with a coach company at Bognor Regis known as Worthing Motor Services, having acquired the business of a Mr. Davis, of Bognor. From the summer of 1916 it ran a service to Portsmouth for the summer period only then in October, 1919, it applied for licences to run into Portsmouth on a more regular basis. In an attempt to protect the substantial investment that the Corporation had made in the tramway system, a minimum fare was imposed by the Watch Committee when it granted a licence. This was to lead to many arguments which went on to the outbreak of the Second World War and ended in a formal co-ordination agreement in 1946. By April, 1920, a regular service between Brighton and Southsea was operating, running through Havant, Drayton and Cosham.

The increasing competition between Southsea and Horndean prompted the Corporation and the Portsdown and Horndean Light Railway to enter into an agreement for joint running, allowing Horndean — or Green Cars, as they were known — to run from Horndean, through Waterlooville, Cosham, North End, Guildhall, and Palmerston Road to Canoe Lake.

One of the independent operators running buses outside Portsmouth was the Denmead Queen Bus Service which used a Thornycroft on a route from Hambledon to the Town Hall via Denmead and Waterlooville.
(C.H.T. Marshall)

Mr. Spaven, the former manager had been concerned about the competition and in 1923 had suggested buying the Portsdown and Horndean Light Railway. He also recommended the introduction of "rail-less vehicles", trolley buses, and extending services to Havant and Fareham. At the same time, a new depot was proposed, although this was not a new idea: a similar plan to build one in the Bransbury Park area of Eastney had been made but the ground was unsuitable.

Following the borough boundary extension to Drayton, from July, 1925, various services, usually routes to Cosham, were sent on to Drayton. The fares were lower than those of Southdown, which had applied to the Watch Committee to run services to East Cosham, Drayton and Wymering. The committee wanted to impose various conditions to guard the interests of the Corporation.

A 2d protective fare on all fares south of Cosham railway gates was proposed, meaning the equivalent 1d tram fare would have been a 3d bus ride on Southdown. A minimum 6d fare imposed in 1919 had been abandoned for a 3d minimum, however, the 6d minimum was re-introduced later.

Sample fares in January 1923:

	Southdown	Corporation	1986
Guildhall to North End	3d	1½d	32p
Guildhall to Cosham	4d	3d	38p
Guildhall to Drayton	5d	n/a	44p

The Corporation argued that it needed to protect its investment, particularly as there was an outstanding debt of about £200,000 on the tramway network, due to the extensive track repairs. There were those who argued that Southdown with its upholstered seats gave a better service, and it was faster — a trip by bus to the Guildhall from Cosham taking 18 minutes, compared with the 25 minutes of a tram. Southdown officials admitted they were out to compete with the Corporation with buses were accused of obstructing trams and poaching passengers at shelters. In its annual report of June, 1927, Southdown announced a profit of £50,000 and was able to pay a dividend to shareholders.

The Editorial of the *Evening News* gave a balanced view of the situation: the Corporation had an investment to protect but the needs of the public had to be considered. The trams had given good service, carrying some 40,000,000 passengers a year but the vehicles were deteriorating. Leaking roofs, causing passengers to stand in the lower saloon because of wet seats, did not go down well. One passenger travelling from the Guildhall to Milton on a rainy night tried to put up his umbrella while standing in the lower saloon, the downpour inside the tram was so bad. Womén complained of being pushed aside at tram stops by men who were not prepared to travel on the top deck of an open tram.

On April 1, 1931, the Road Traffic Act (1930) was introduced, bringing some form of centralised control over public transport, whereby an operator had to apply for a licence to run on a set route at a pre-determined timetable with pre-set fares. Under the Construction and Use Regulations of Public Service Vehicles, regular examinations of the vehicles was ordered and certificates of fitness introduced with provision to examine buses at regular intervals. Set dimensions for seats and gangway widths, step heights etc. were all part of the construction regulations and the licensing of drivers and conductors was introduced.

The Act gave the Corporation authority to run services to its own boundaries, provided it obtained a licence from the Traffic Commissioners, who had taken over from the Watch Committee. The borough boundary was Drayton but from April 1, 1932, it was extended to Portsdown Road at Portchester to the west and Rectory Avenue at Farlington in the east but remained to the north at Widley. Several attempts had been made by the Corporation to run a service to Drayton but had been thwarted by Southdown.

The Corporation applied to run services to Farlington, Portchester, Cosham, Wymering, Fareham and Purbrook Common. Again, there followed a barrage of correspondence in the *Evening News,* which gave the Traffic Commissioners' hearing good coverage. Farlington people did not want the Corporation buses, they were happy with Southdown. Portchester had similar views and concern was expressed at the high rate of fatal accidents. It was claimed that as many as 34 people had been killed in one year on Portsmouth Road, Portchester. For example, in 1931, five fatal accidents are recorded in the office diary.

The arguments went on. Eventually, the Corporation withdrew its application to run to Purbrook because of its agreement with the Portsdown and Horndean Light Railway.

In January, 1934, the Traffic Commissioners refused the Corporation application, the Chairman stating that the area was adequately covered by Southdown. A Mr. Woodward, who had represented the Corporation at the hearing, is quoted as saying: "They (Southdown) had soft seats on their buses and hard heads on their management."

With the appointment of Captain W.E. Hudd as Official City Guide in January, 1933, the Corporation made an application to run city tours on a similar route to today's 101 service, except for Eastern Road and the motorway. The attraction then, as now, was the magnificent view from Portsdown Hill, Objections were raised and the application failed but the Chairman of the Traffic Commissioners suggested Captain Hudd might apply in his own right.

In July, 1934, Southdown sought the renewal of its licences from South Parade Pier to South Harting, Westbourne, Emsworth, Petersfield, Horndean (two services), Warsash, Fareham, and Hayling Island, and North End to the Dockyard. In a form of retaliation, the Corporation objected to the renewal, requesting the usual protective fare, and asked that Southdown be stopped from picking up passengers between Cosham and South Parade Pier. The objection failed, except for the protective fares.

Eventually, the Corporation was allowed to operate beyond Cosham Railway Gates to the Red Lion. This remained until the outbreak of the Second World War when emergency measures came into being. From January 1, 1930, another agreement between the Corporation and Southdown was implemented. Southdown buses ran over Corporation tram routes charging tram fares but the Corporation received all the revenue earned within the city boundary and Southdown was paid a fixed sum per mile operated.

This agreement was in force for two years until the Corporation realised it was losing money. From January 1, 1932, a protective fare was introduced again. This was 3d up to a 1d stage and 4d up to a 3d stage but north of North End it was graduated down to the same level from Hilsea.

Protective fares remained in operation until May, 1947, when a co-ordination agreement between the Corporation and Southdown, prompted by the Regional Traffic Commissioners, took effect. The basis of the agreement was that the Corporation provided 57 per cent. of mileage and took 57 per cent. of the receipts and Southdown the remainder of each in an area bounded by Fareham, Petersfield and Emsworth.

The agreement was revised in 1967 but the 1985 Transport Act made the arrangement difficult to continue unless it was ratified by the Office of Fair Trading. It was felt the agreement in its entirety would not be allowed. The 1985 Act does permit working arrangements between operators but not the rigid ones detailed in the Joint Operating Agreement.

Trams or buses?

Through the columns of the *Evening News*, two correspondents carried on a discussion. One stated that trams were better than buses. He enjoyed his morning ride on the top deck, it was "most invigorating". The reply came back that to ride on an open-top tram he would need "pluck, the hide of an elephant and a bottle of embrocation afterwards". That writer kept in trim by sparring for a famous hard-hitting heavyweight prize-fighter — he enjoyed this more than travelling on a tram.

An unpopular walk

At the Traffic Commissioners' hearing into the extension of services, the Corporation Engineer and General Manager, Mr.Ben Hall, was cross-examined by the Chairman as to why the Corporation should extend its routes, in particular to the Red Lion public house at Cosham. With his dry, Yorkshire wit, Mr.Hall replied:" Sir, the local men do not like to walk to the Red Lion." Exclaimed the Chairman: "But, it's a well-known hostelry." Mr.Hall: "Yes sir, but they don't like to walk home from the Red Lion to their homes either."

CHAPTER V

ON THE BUSES

Who was the first Portsmouth Corporation bus driver? An article in the *Evening News* of April, 1969, answers the question — Mr. A.E. Budd, of Copnor.

In 1969, he was 90 years old and still Managing Director of Southsea Ideal Mineral Waters Ltd. The article covered a reunion of three former employees of the department, Mr. Archie Fielder, who started work with the department as a conductor and finally became General Manager in 1965 and retired in 1968, Mr. R. (Cherry) Perkins and Mr. Budd.

Mr. Budd and Mr. Perkins were two of the first recruits for driving the first buses bought by the Corporation. Cherry Perkins wrote down his recollections in a hand-written autobiography now held by the City Museums. After demob from the First World War, he was waiting to join the queue at the Labour Exchange when he overheard two men talking about the Corporation buying buses and probably wanting drivers. Cherry went to the transport office, then at the Guldhall, and asked to see the General Manager. Much to his surprise, he was given an interview without an appointment. The vacancies for drivers were supposed to be a well-kept secret — nothing ever changes. In due course, Cherry was engaged, after giving details of his war service driving various forms of Army transport. In 1919, mechanics and drivers were held in the same regard that computer programmers and technicians are today.

Billy Budd had driven trams for the Corporation after the war. Later, he was asked to drive a bus and he claimed to be the first bus driver in a vehicle from Vivash Road to North End depot.

The Thornycrofts with Wadham Stringer bodies were delivered in July, 1919. The chassis were ex-War Department and had been built originally to see service in France with the Army for troop transport. There are believed to be four remaining in the world today. The original bodies were replaced later by former London General Omnibus Company bodies.

The first temporary route was from North End to Clarence Pier and South Parade Pier, probably as part of the 1919 peace celebrations. The first permanent 15-minute service started on August 11 on a route known as M from Devonshire Avenue to the Dockyard and back along St Mary's Road to the prison.

Cherry Perkins recalled the poor state of the roads; Jessie Road, Southsea, being made up of granite blocks was particularly bad. For most of his seven years bus driving Cherry had a regular conductor, Harry Thorpe. On one occasion, travelling on the muddy road, Cherry went over a bump and Harry fell off the back platform into the mud. In wind, rain and driving snow, the only protection for drivers was a canvas roll.

From February, 1920, the service frequency was ten minutes from midday to 8 p.m., then 15-minutes. The all-round fare was 1d. Less than a year later, the 1d and 2d fares were abolished. On May 25, 1926, the Thornycrofts operated a service to Portsdown Hill for Easter Bank Holiday. In August, 1921, a bus service from Eastney to Cosham along Copnor Road started but, as private operators had found, it was not profitable. By October, it was reduced to travelling to Stubbington Avenue and ceased on November 13. The carrying of parcels and baggage as a service to anyone requiring it commenced in February, 1921.

The office diary for February, 1923, records buses travelling through Arundel Street, Landport. Until it was redeveloped, Arundel Street was to cause many problems; at one section, two buses were unable to pass each other.

June, 1924, saw the introduction of the Guy Runabout toast rack buses bought for the seafront service. They were withdrawn after the Second World War and one was destroyed in the air raid on Eastney depot but a chassis of one was used as a trailer. A third was converted to a cash van immediately after the war. They

The Southsea seafront service between Clarence Pier and Ferry Road used a Guy runabout which was popular on sunny days. The driver/conductor pictured originally had been a tram points boy. *(A. Moody)*

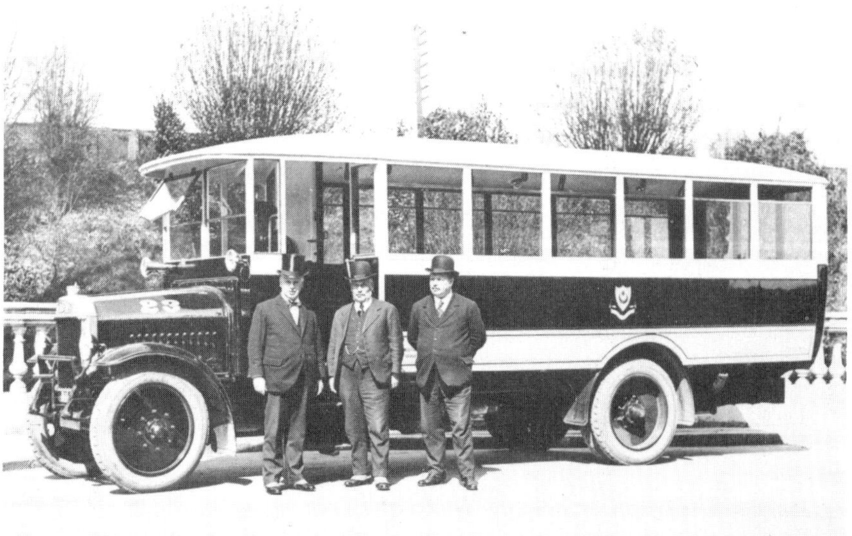

A Dennis 26-seater front entrance bus was accepted with due ceremony in 1925. They were first used on the Eastney to Alexandra Park and Eastney to Cosham and Drayton services. *(C.P.P.T.D.)*

were all delivered on small solid-tyred wheels and these were changed to the more-conventional pneumatic tyres in 1929.

Between June and July, 1924, the first single deck one-man operated buses were delivered. The service to Cosham was introduced again but now started from South Parade Pier.

Demolition of the Jessie Road railway bridge in February, 1925, created problems for the M service which had to be diverted. A further ten single-deckers were delivered between April 16 and 25, to provide new services. These were used on a route from the junction of Copnor Road and Stubbington Avenue along Chichester Road and back to Copnor via Laburnum Grove. This was extended later to Alexandra Park.

The first incursion beyond Cosham railway gates was when the South Parade Pier to Cosham service was extended to Drayton on July 12, 1925. On September 1, a turnround was agreed at the New Inn, Drayton, but the service was stopped two days later.

It recommenced on November 9, 1925, and was known as the H-route, running a 15-minute service until 1 p.m., then a ten-minute frequency. Mr. Gordon Privett, who for many years has been involved in the coaching business in Portsmouth, recalls the Dennis E type buses turning at the side of the New Inn. There was a large corner stone on the wall of the pub that was just the right height to catch mudguards. Every one of the Dennis had a bent front wing in a very short time.

There is a mystery about the A.E.C. B-type bus, fleet number 35 which the office diary for September, 1928, records: "London General Omnibus Committee bus licensed by Public Vehicles Committee fleet no. 35." The chassis of this A.E.C. B-type was converted for carrying petrol in August, 1927, but there is no other record as to what happened to this vehicle and, so far, a photograph of this type has eluded all collectors.

For the remainder of the 1920s, experimental services were tried: the Drayton service from Eastney was via Copnor Road, then changed on its return run through Commercial Road, King's Road, Grove Road, and Palmerston Road to South Parade Pier.

Eastern Road was built as far as the Airport Service Road and was known then as the road to nowhere but it was popular as a day out and was used for car racing on several occasions. From April, 1927, two buses ran a service from Palmerston Road via Velder Avenue to the golf links at Great Salterns.

The first forward-control buses bought by the Corporation were Dennis E Types with Ransome's bodies in 1927. *(C.P.P.T.D.)*

Former bus fleet number 61 in a sorry condition in a scrapyard after service with a fairground operator. *(A.M. Lambert)*

A type of vehicle new to Portsmouth operated in June/July, 1927. Two Karrier single-deckers arrived on June 13 and three double-deck Karriers on July 9. These went into service on July 14 when the fourth one joined the fleet. In 1927 these three-axle 60-seater closed top double-decker buses were very futuristic. The enclosed cab and top deck were a welcome luxury for driver and passengers. The reason for two rear axles was that legislation limited the weight for each axle to six tons — now ten tons — because of the lack of technology in making pneumatic tyres. The major advances in bus engineering and comfort within ten years had led to the demise of the ailing Thornycrofts.

Unfortunately, the life of the Karriers was short. They proved to be expensive to operate, the modern term would be "gas guzzlers", and mechanically they were very troublesome. They were used on a service from South Parade Pier to the George public house at the top of Portsdown Hill. No doubt, the journey up the hill took its toll on the engines. As an apprentice with Chesterfield Corporation, the author remembers older men talking about the rear axle problems of the Karriers operated by that authority. The last Karriers arrived in Portsmouth in late August, 1928; number 44 was damaged while being delivered. By 1936, the city's Karriers had passed into the history books with the trams.

A group of twin rear axle Karriers made such an impressive sight outside the Guildhall when they were delivered in 1928 that the manufacurers used the photograph in advertisements. *(C.P.P.T.D.)*

The driver and conductor of Karrier fleet Number 40 proudly stand in front of their newly-delivered vehicle at Cosham terminus in 1927. The unmade surface of Copnor Road caused many problems with the tranmissions of these buses. *(C. Phillips)*

Only two single-deckers by Karrier company were bought by the Department. This one is fleet Number 38. *(C.P.P.T.D.)*

A new service, known as the E and F route, between Alexandra Park and Eastney via Gladys Avenue, North End, Copnor Bridge and White House started in November, 1927, using single-deck Dennis buses.

The first recorded instance of private hire started at the same time when the Education Committee chartered two buses each day to take children to and from the Futcher School of Recovery at Drayton, the charge being 6d (2½p) a head.

By 1928, the department owned 60 buses in addition to the trams. Several temporary garages were rented in the town to house them. Vivash Road power station site was converted to a bus depot when the electric power for the trams was provided by the Portsmouth Corporation Electricity Department. There was a serious need for improving maintenance and garaging space for the buses and a temporary shed was built at Eastney in about 1928 on the site of the existing depot at the rear of what is now Eastney Health Centre.

When the existing depot was built, this so-called temporary one became the permanent way shed where for a period tramlines were stored and crossings and junctions were laid out for trial before being installed. Eventually, a covered metal and uniform stores was built under its roof and for the Second World War an air raid shelter was erected in this shed. When the whole of the building was demolished in the late-1970s, several interesting photographs were found, some of which have been used in this book.

A sub-committee, including the General Manager and committee Chairman, visited Liverpool, Leeds and Chesterfield in April, 1928, where new depots had been built. The one at Chesterfield, where the author started work as an apprentice in 1957, was put up in 1927 and at that time the roof over the parking area was the largest unsupported span in England. Following their visits, the sub-committee recommended that a new bus and tram depot be built. Started in 1929, the building incorporated all the latest facilites of the time. The garage was divided into two sections, one for buses and one for trams. The tramlines in the east end of the depot still remain as do the former pits which were covered over with steel mesh and concrete but left unfilled to ease drainage.

The buses of the mid-1920s to mid-1930s were not very reliable or economical on fuel. During the period up to 1935 buses of a variety of manufacturers were bought for trial — Dennis, Thornycroft, Tilling Stevens, Crossley, A.E.C., and Leyland.

The Dennis E.V. single-decker, fleet Number 63, had a rear door for passengers. The photograph was taken before delivery in 1929. *(C.P.P.T.D.)*

The only new A.E.C. double-decker bought by the Department ws destroyed in the air raid on Eastney depot in March, 1941. Its engine and gearbox were sold to Nottingham City Transport. *(T.H. Dethridge)*

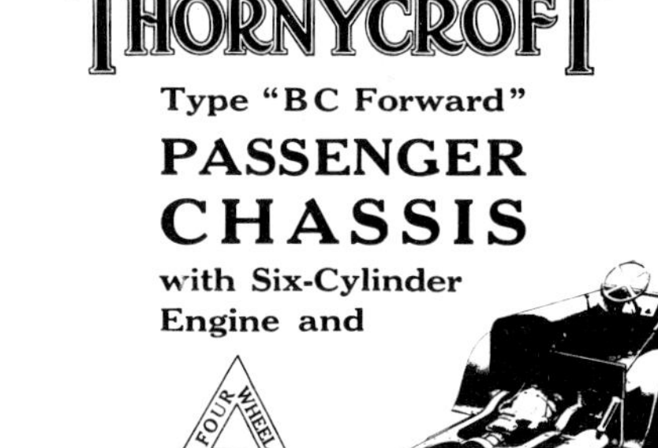

Two Thornycrofts, fleet Numbers 72 and 71, wait to take workers from the Dockyard home to North End and Alexandra Park. *(C.P.P.T.D.)*

Regarded by many as the best single-deck bus of the times, the Leyland Lion chassis was popular with coach operators in the 1930s. Fleet Number 3, Leyland Lion L.T.2 with a Park Royal body, was the only one bought by Portsmouth Corporation. *(J.E. Gull)*

The new Tilling Stevens line up outside Eastney depot in the shadow of the tramway they were soon to replace. *(C.P.P.T.D.)*

Resplendent in its new livery, the Tilling Stevens (fleet Number 80), set a style which would be followed for 30 years. *(C.P.P.T.D.)*

In 1934, Mr. Hall decided to buy Leyland's model T.D.4 with the order for the vehicles' bodies divided between the English Electric Company and Cravens, of Sheffield. The one A.E.C. Regent bought in 1931 was given the same fleet number, 35, as the B-type A.E.C. of 1927.

The Crossley Conders were not very successful as they were unstable when braking in heavy rain. In spite of this, one was converted to a recovery vehicle by having the chassis shortened, a crane fitted and a purpose-built crew compartment installed. Fortunately, this vehicle was saved from the breakers' yard and is now in storage at Fort Purbrook waiting for a place in a museum. It is the only Crossley Conder remaining in the country.

The Tilling Stevens buses also had flaws, although, for the period, they were rather attractive. So much so that two Royal Marines from Eastney Barracks stole one from the depot. It was found on its way to London, minus its top deck, because the Marines had gone under a low bridge. For the remainder of its life, bus number 80 was used for tree lopping, an essential job to protect the roofs of double-deckers from being damaged by overhanging trees.

The roof of fleet Number 80 was removed unofficially when two Royal Marines stole the bus from Eastney depot to got to London but they took a wrong turning and went under the railway bridge at Fareham. The vehicle was later converted for tree lopping. *(J.E. Gull)*

A Crossley Condor bus, Number 74, was converted into a breakdown lorry. Believed to be the only remaining Condor, it is now in storage at Fort Widley on Portsdown Hill waiting for restoration. *(J. Dorey)*

A Leyland T.D.2 in Methuen Road at the rear of Eastney depot. The ornate gates on the right were used at North End depot from 1902. *(C.P.P.T.D.)*

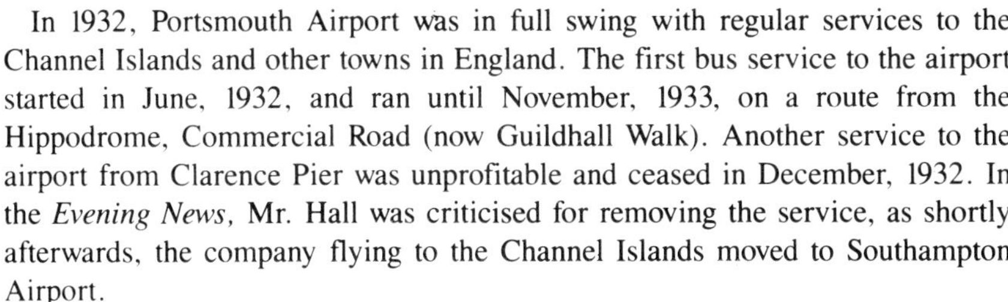

In 1932, Portsmouth Airport was in full swing with regular services to the Channel Islands and other towns in England. The first bus service to the airport started in June, 1932, and ran until November, 1933, on a route from the Hippodrome, Commercial Road (now Guildhall Walk). Another service to the airport from Clarence Pier was unprofitable and ceased in December, 1932. In the *Evening News,* Mr. Hall was criticised for removing the service, as shortly afterwards, the company flying to the Channel Islands moved to Southampton Airport.

Twelve Leyland T.D.2 chassis with English Electric bodies were delivered in July, 1933; the chassis cost £979 each and the body, £670. The cost of a modern bus chassis is £70,000 to £75,000.

May, 1932, was the first occasion when buses were sold on a formal basis for scrap to a commercial vehicle clearing house. The 19 Dennis single-deckers were withdrawn from service after only eight years on the road, whereas the modern bus has a life expectancy of 20 years. Fourteen Dennis buses were sold to the clearing house and the remaining five were converted to lorries with one as a tower wagon for overhead line repairs.

Leyland Titan TD2 at Cosham compound. The banking and bridge behind the bus were for the track of the Portsdown and Horndean Light Railway. Fleet Number 18, converted to a tower wagon, T.W.2, is now owned by Mr. John Dorey. *(J. Dorey)*

Pictured at South Parade Pier, Southsea, fleet Number 100, a Crossley Condor. The photograph was presented to the Department by the family of the driver. (C.P.P.T.D.)

The 1930s Leyland buses which were sold in the 1950s had a low scrap value as the bodies were wooden-framed. In the 1960s, double-deck buses were sold for as little as £75. Some were bought by major civil engineering contractors for staff transport and others went to travelling showmen as mobile homes and equipment stores.

A batch of 20 Crossley Condors arrived in July and August of 1932, following the success of the Crossley bought in 1931.

Diesel engines, or, as they were then known, oil engines for buses were in the early stages of development. The petrol engine had reigned supreme but it was very expensive to run, fuel consumption being as low as 4 m.p.g. The new diesel engine was more efficient with consumption of 8 to 9 m.p.g. and on long journeys 12 to 13 m.p.g. was common. A penalty was that exhaust fumes could be most objectionable. On several occasions Mr. Hall was taken to task and asked to address meetings of ratepayers' organisations. One resident of Methuen Road, near Eastney depot, wrote to the *Evening News* complaining and sent a photograph of the street blacked out with exhaust fumes.

As part of the replacement programme for the trams, 40 Leyland Titan T.D.4s were ordered with delivery spread from November, 1936, to February, 1937. They were to prove very successful, remaining in service until the late 1950s, the last being withdrawn in 1963 and four were converted to open-toppers.

Up to the start of the war in 1939, many service changes took place with trolley buses replacing trams and buses. The greyhound stadium operated its own bus service to Stamshaw in 1933 on Mondays, Wednesdays, Fridays and Saturdays. Conductors issued tickets for travelling and admission to the track at one shilling (5p) and two shillings (10p). The Corporation charged the stadium £2 for a double-decker and 30s (£1.50) for a single-decker.

A one-way system for buses was introduced in Cosham High Street for two reasons: the north end of the street is very narrow and the level crossing at the south end caused considerable delays to all the traffic. All buses travelling north went up Cosham High Street and those going south had to use Northern Road.

A tower wagon was converted from a Dennis E Type single-decker bus but due to the unreliability of the Dennis engine, one from a Tilling Stevens double-decker was fitted during the conversion. (C.P.P.T.D.)

What a karry-on

Frank Holmes, an active member of the retired employees association, tells of an occasion when he was working on Karriers travelling from Eastney to Cosham along Copnor Road, then a gravel-surfaced road. Travelling along at 20 m.p.h., there was an almighty bang, the bus ground to a halt and they found the propshaft between the two rear axles had broken and come up through the floor of the bus.

Fleet Number 130, a Leyland Titan T.D.4 chassis with a body by Leyland, pictured at Cosham. Only four of this combination of chassis and body were bought by the Corporation. (J. Dorey)

Lost and found

Charges for lost property being returned to their rightful owner, with a reward to the conductor, were introduced in 1933. Unfortunately, problems with lost property do occur, when the conductor or driver/conductor finds lost property on his bus. He is required to check the contents of a purse or handbag and must count any money and list the items, which does cause embarrassing situations but it is necessary. Umbrellas and odd gloves are very popular items left on buses. Items not claimed are stored for one year and eventually sold by auction, the proceeds going to the sick and benevolent society. When the children's television programme "Blue Peter" collected keys for one of its annual appeals, the department contributed a large box of brass keys.

The Leyland T.D.4 chassis was used with bodies by Cravens, of Sheffield. Fleet Number 131 was one of 29 of the vehicles which operated in Portsmouth from 1936 to the mid-1950s. (J. Dorey)

Foreign travels

Redundant Portsmouth buses have been sold to other operators in this country and abroad, including Devon and Cornwall, the Midlands and Sheffield. One bus sold in 1981 now operates in Australia.

Some of the first single-deckers the author was involved in selling in 1976 went to Mauritius. Six months later, the department received a letter from a native written in Pidgin English applying for a job as a motor mechanic. He had found the address from the side of the bus. Before the vehicle left Portsmouth just one coat of paint had been put over the name and address legally required on the lower panel.

"No Spitting"

The notice to passengers in every bus that, no doubt, many people found offensive was "No Spitting" or "Spitting Strictly Forbidden". The need for such notices was emphasised by an incident recorded in the office diary for March 29, 1937. Conductor Barrett remonstrated with a passenger for vomiting on bus number 125 and was struck on the side of the head, causing unconsciousness for a short period. The case was heard in court on May 27, 1937, and a Mr.Hunter was fined £3 for assault, £1 for impeding the conductor and costs of one shilling (5p).

CHAPTER VI

THE DECLINE OF THE TRAM

As well as competition from the more-comfortable buses, the trams operation was experiencing difficulties, with the relaying of tracks causing major disturbances all over the city, particularly in Fratton Road.

Tramlines purchased originally for Copnor Road were not used there but taken to other places in the town for the major renovation of the tramway. Residents had complained about noise of cleaning and grinding from the maintenance of the tramlines at night and this was stopped, so accelerating the decline of the tracks.

Leaking roofs and the general poor condition of the trams, most of which had been in service for 25 years led Mr. Spaven to start a programme of refurbishing the cars. Some of the older trams were extensively rebuilt with vestibules, a glass front to protect the driver and upholstered seats. Mr. Hall agreed that the fleet had come to the end of its useful life and he was responsible for designing a new type of fully-enclosed tramcar which had better suspension and generally was more comfortable.

Mr. Hall's tramcar Number 1 went into regular service on October 9, 1930, the body built by Corporation staff in the workshops at North End. It was capable of travelling at 60 m.p.h. along London Road beyond the Green Posts public house.

The tramways water car and rail grinder used for track maintenance was so well built that its water tanks are still in used at Eastney depot. (C.P.P.T.D.)

Just before the closure of the system in 1936, Number 1 was sold to Sunderland and gave many more years service there

In April, 1931, Fawcett Road, Southsea, was reconstructed and the rails taken up. Two routes were affected — the then 3/4 and 13/14 — the latter being revised and then withdrawn altogether some months later. The 3/4 service was diverted and the section between Fratton Bridge and South Parade Pier was replaced by a single-decker bus service.

As early as November, 1929, bills were posted at half-mile intervals on trampoles stating that the Corporation would be seeking authorisation to include in its next Act permission to run trackless vehicles — trolley buses.

One clear indication of the strength of the anti-tram movement was that at several locations the original stone setts were replaced with wooden blocks to reduce noise levels, particularly at public buildings and sensitive areas. The blocks were a useful source of firewood for residents when they were removed eventually.

In spite of the protective fare, the competition from Southdown was considerable. Several correspondents to the *Evening News* stated that the drivers were more polite than the Corporation ones. The weekly returns printed in the newspaper were

The body of tramcar Number 1 was designed and built by Tramways Department staff. It was capable of speeds of more than 50 m.p.h. (C.P.P.T.D.)

The truck, or chassis, of tramcar Number 1 on the traversing machine at North End depot. The body of Number 1 can be seen in the workshops before being fitted to the chassis. Number 1 was sold to Sunderland Corporation Tramways in 1935 and operated there until 1953. (C.P.P.T.D.)

An arrangement of two seats and a single seat in a row was common inside trams as these views of the interior of tramcar Number 1 show.

showing a drop in revenue on the trams: the figures for November 1932 show that the takings for the trams were about £300 down and the buses £560 up in one week compared with the previous year.

A correspondent to the *Evening News* wrote that he always let a tram go by to catch a bus as he preferred to be set down on the pavement rather than in the middle of a stream of traffic. He described the trams as an antiquated collection of uncomfortable thunderboxes.

In February, 1934, Mr. Hall itemised the financial situation. The net loss for the year 1932-33 was estimated at £5,168, and the estimated deficit for March 31, 1935, was put at £16,000, giving the total loss of £21,168.

Mr. Hall's reasons for the deficit were: "Hurtful competition by privately-owned service";

"The increase of the capital charges due to the acquisition of receiving new buses and the modernising of the fleet (trams)";

"The loss of traffic to the tramways section, due to the preference of the riding public for the newer medium, the buses";

"A general trade depression and an overall shortage of money".

The City Treasurer had indicated that the total deficit could be reversed by a levy on the rates of 4d in the pound in one year. At that time, the half crown rate (2s6d, 12p) was uppermost in the minds of many local politicians.

Generally, the cost of transport in Portsmouth had remained static since the First World War but there had been a shortening of stages, which was used as a means of increasing revenue. The working expenses since the war had increased by 95 per cent., in spite of reductions of 1s (5p) per week in pay for the workers.

In the year ending March, 1923, there had been a surplus of £20,000 and during the period of minimum fares imposed on Southdown, July, 1927 to December, 1929, the financial situation improved. The year ending March, 1929, showed a surplus of £37,182 but by 1933 the deficit was £8,168.

Mr. Hall's report went on to give the committee the options it could take to overcome the deficit problems. The total revenue of the department could be increased by raising fares. With almost one-third of the income from 1d fares — half of the annual 58 million passengers paid 1d fare — it was a difficult situation as a 1/2d or 50 per cent. increase would have caused an outcry. Any bus fare rises needed the approval of the Traffic Commissioners but this did not apply to tramway or trolley bus services at the time.

The Westminster company of David Rowell built the elaborate tramway shelters alongside the south side of the Guildhall in Park Road. *(C.P.P.T.D.)*

Later bus shelters in the same position, installed about 1955, provided less protection from the weather. *(C.P.P.T.D.)*

For a ld fare, a distance of 1.22 miles could be travelled and Mr. Hall suggested that the stage length be reduced to 0.9 mile, which would give extra income of £17,000 a year. The introduction of prepaid season tickets, the forerunner of today's Travelcard, was put forward but it was pointed out the department sold £14,000-worth of prepaid tickets, which cost £2,000 in lost revenue. Transfer tickets with their attendant administrative problems and possible loss of income were also suggested.

Capital costs of running the service were high, too — £24,000 for trams and £33,800 for buses; rates were over £9,000 a year, maintaining the roadways cost £10,000 annually and central administration charges of the Town Clerk's and City Treasurer's staff were higher than many other local authorities.

Mr. Hall's conclusion was that full consideration should be given to the substitution of tramsways by the more-modern trolley bus. But there was still the outstanding debt on the tramway that had to be resolved.

When the report was made public, considerable debate followed and public meetings were held by various organisations.

At a public meeting in April, 1932, Councillor Pearson forecast a remodelling of the Transport Department within three years. He outlined the virtues of the department, giving £138,500 in rate relief and paying £235,654 in ordinary rates. Over £80,000 had been paid to the national exchequer and the tramways had provided employment to over 1,000 people for many years.

The following month, the Chairman of the Tramways Committee, Sir John Timpson, met members of Portsmouth Chamber of Trade and defended the tramways, leading to further correspondence in the Evening News. A Mr. Thomas wrote saying that all vehicles should be made to go more slowly to give tram drivers and conductors better time at their work. At that time, Northern Parade, Hilsea, was under construction and Mr. Thomas, fearing it would become a racetrack, suggested trams should run in that road. He lost that argument but he was right about the racetrack.

Mr. Hall answered the "sell to a private company" critics by pointing out the prime consideration of the private companies would be their shareholders.

From his report of February, 1934, the decision to close the tramway system was eventually taken. The original plan was to spread this changeover across ten years but in reality two years was found to be adequate.

The changeover gave many problems such as the necessity for two overhead wires for trolley buses compared with the single wire for trams. The work of erecting new overhead wires would need to go on while maintaining a service; tramlines would have to be taken up with many others left under tarmacadam — some are still visible today. All tram drivers would need to learn how to drive buses or trolley buses. Some did, those who did not worked in the depot until retirement, except men over 60 years old and they were able to retire on a pension.

Up to 1936, the trolley head, the piece of equipment which picked up the electricity from the overhead wire, had been fixed. For the transition period, all trams were fitted with a swivelling trolley head.

In the narrow streets the trams had to use the positive trolley bus wires as they were erected, changing to the independent tramway wires on wide roads where the trolley bus wire deviated from the track. Bamboo poles were bought to be used for changing the swivel head from one wire to another, superseding the use of a trailing cord. Tramcar Number 84, now in store at Eastney Depot, still has its trailing cord. At least two of the bamboo poles are also at the depot, used for opening and closing windows in the workshops.

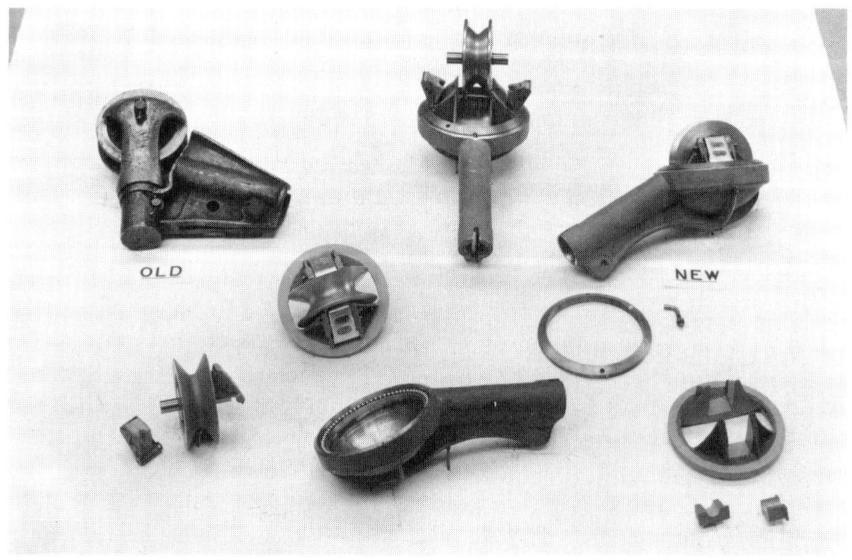

The old trolley heads caused excessive wear on the overhead cable, particularly at corners, so the swivel, or unfoulable, head which was introduced during the installation of overhead cable for trolley buses was a big improvement. (C.P.P.T.D.)

Following the strong protests by passengers, tramcars numbers 55, 57, 64 and 80 were rebuilt in 1930 and the covered-top cars had some renovation work carried out. In 1932, older trams with open tops, numbers 44, 45, 19, 69 and 85, were rebuilt and these were the last to be disposed of. Others not refurbished were broken up at Eastney and North End depots, the frameworks sold for firewood, to make room for the delivery of buses and trolley buses.

Further refurbishing of tramcars continued in 1933, 1934 and 1935, as the replacement programme should have been spread over ten years. It was reasonable to expect trams to be running until well into the 1940s. Tramcars numbers 12, 17 and 56 were rebuilt in 1933 and numbers 48, 73, 49 and 10 in 1934. In 1935, number 11 was the last to be rebuilt and was the same as number 10. These had vestibule screens fitted, modified staircases, straight side panels and driver's safety blinds. Ironically, numbers 10 and 11 were the first tramcars to be refurbished under Mr. Spaven's smartening-up programme of 1920 and they were the last under Mr. Hall's scheme.

By October, 1936, the tram fleet had been reduced; the only tramcars in use were the rebuilt open-tops and the 12 covered ones. Extensive renovation work had been done on cars numbers 36, 51, 29, 24 and 43. Air push bells had been fitted to replace the rod that went through the tramcar ending in a hammer that rang a bell on the driver's platform.

On the first of that month trolley buses ran on the service between Clarence Pier, Southsea, and the Red Lion at Cosham, via the Guildhall and North End, similar to the 1 and 2 service of today. The two Copnor via Lake Road routes were changed to trolley buses from November 1, leaving the 5/6 and 17/18 to Eastney and Milton — similar to those of today — as the only tram services

Finally, at 11.45 a.m. on Tuesday, November 10, 1936, four of the covered-top trams, suitably decorated, travelled in convoy led by car number 106, driven initially by Sir John Timpson. For the final section of the journey, the driver was the Lord Mayor, Councillor Spickernell. The front indicator showed "Journey's End" and the rear "Speed With Comfort". The route number boxes displayed "1901 - 1936". The other trams had "Special" on their indicators. Commemorative tickets were issued to all passengers.

The *Evening News* reported the event in great detail: "Just before midday, the four cars loaded with passengers proceeded from the Guildhall Square at funeral pace. As the procession passed the meat market in Greetham Street, the butchers

Staff of the Tramways Department found time for some social life, including the foundation of a band in about 1920. (C.P.P.T.D.)

CITY OF PORTSMOUTH
PASSENGER TRANSPORT DEPARTMENT

1901 —— 1936

SOUVENIR TICKET
available on the
last journey run by
ELECTRIC TRAMCAR
:: in the ::
CITY OF PORTSMOUTH
From: The Guildhall *To:* Eastney
on
TUESDAY, 10th NOVEMBER, 1936
at 11.45 a.m.

Lord Mayor: Councillor F. J. Spickernell
Deputy Lord Mayor: Alderman W. J. Avens
Chairman Passenger Transport Committee:
Alderman Sir John Timpson, K.B.E., J.P.
Vice-Chairman: Councillor W. S. R. Pugsley
General Manager & Engineer: Mr. Ben Hall
[P.T.O.

stood at the doorways of their stores and clanged their cleavers, which were suspended on ropes from beams.

"The last car was fitted with loudspeakers and a record player, playing:- Dear old pal, jolly old pal, we've been together in all sorts of weather."

Along the route through Blackfriars Road, Victoria Road, Albert Road and then Highland Road crowds gathered. As the procession passed through Albert Road, "Pomp and Circumstance" was played and when it neared the depot there were strains of the "Death and Glory" march. When the last tram came to a halt, the tramways department band played "Auld Lang Syne".

Thus, with due ceremony the last tram was "put to bed" for the last time, ending 35 years of tram operation by the Corporation. The trams were followed by the new trolley buses on the 17/18 and 5/6 routes.

The civic party and guests returned to the Guildhall for lunch to which some of the former horse-tram drivers were invited. On a later occasion, Sir John Timpson met many of the tram drivers at a social gathering at the Tramways Club to express his gratitude for all their loyalty over the years.

Portsmouth Rock

A woman wrote to the tramways department complaining about the condition of tramcars relating that her niece who was on holiday from the north of England wanted some Portsmouth rock to take home. The aunt stated that she took her niece on a tram ride round Portsmouth and now she had enough rock to last her the rest of her life. Another woman wrote suggesting the purchase of secondhand tramcars. Apparently, she had been to Plymouth where secondhand cars bought from Exeter were used and they were in much better condition than the Portsmouth tramcars.

Learning the ropes

Bill Pornicott was one of the tram conductors who put a tram into the water at the floating bridge. As a conductor, his driver let him drive the tram along the High Street, Old Portsmouth, late at night. When he arrived at the end of the line, he asked: "How do you stop this bloody tram?" But it was too late — in he went, tram and all.

In later years, he had a trainee conductor with him when the General Manager, Mr. Ben Hall, was a passenger on their bus but the trainee did not know. When they arrived at the terminus, Mr. Hall and his wife did not leave their seats. The trainee told them to get off, to which Mr. Hall replied: "Do you know who I am? I'm Ben Hall, General Manager." The conductor's response was: "I don't care if you're Town Hall — get off."

CHAPTER VII

HELLO TROLLEY

At the Municipal Tramways Association Conference held in the Guildhall in August, 1923, the General Manager from Birmingham spoke of the virtues of trolley buses. He stated that, being practically noiseless, for ease and comfort of operation, no other vehicle could compare with the trolley. In October, 1923, Mr. Spaven recommended to the Tramways Committee that rail-less vehicles should be used as a replacement for motor vehicles. At this time, the trams were proving to be successful and no strong complaints had been made. Mr. Spaven sugggested they should operate from Cosham to Havant and along Western Road and Southampton Road to Fareham but this was not pursued.

It was seven years later, when complaints about the tramway system were at an all-time high, that the Tramways Committee considered trolley bus operation again. Eventually, in October, 1932, the committee decided to operate an experimental trolley bus route.

During the summer of 1933, members of the Tramways Committee visited other trolley bus operators and manufacturers. Mr. Hall had suggested that a selection of the different types of trolley buses available should be selected for trial. The details of the 15 selected for trial are listed here as they are in the office diary on the days they were delivered to Portsmouth.

1934		
July 10th	Trolley Bus No 14 RV4662 6 wheeler	
	Sunbeam chassis No. 12026S	£1128.10s
	Body 60 seats	£887.00s
	Metroplitan Cammell	£2015.10s
July 16th	Trolley Bus No. 16 R.V. 4663 6 wheeler	
	A.E.C. Chassis No. 663075	£1181.10s
	Cammell Body 60 seats	£887.00s
	Metropolitan	£2068.10s
July 24th	Trolley Bus No. 11 R.V. 4661 4 wheeler	
	Karrier Chassis No. 55005	£1023.8s.9d.
	Metropolitan Cammell Body 50 seater	£883.Os.Od.
		£31856.8s.9d.

Trolley buses pass each other in London Road, Hilsea but the overhead wires and tracks are still in place for trams.
(C.P.P.T.D.)

July 25th	Trolley Bus No. 10 R.V. 4660 4 wheeler	
	Sunbeam chassis No. 13003s.	£1065.00d.
	Metropolitan Cammell Body 50 seater	£833.00d.
		£1898.00d.
July 28th	Trolley Bus. No. 7 R.V. 4655	
	Leyland Chasis TBD2/4548	£1000.14s.
	English Electric Body 50 seater	£785.00d.
		£1785.14s.
July 30th	Trolley Bus No. 5 R.V. 4653	
	Leyland Chassis TBD/4546	£1000.14s
	English Electric Body 50 seater	£785.00d.
		£1785.14s
July 30th	Trolley Bus No. 6 R.V. 4654	
	Leyland Chassis TBD2/4547	
	English Electric Body 50 seats	£1785.14s.
August 5th	Trolley Bus No.13 R.V. 4659	
	Sunbeam 6 wheeler Chassis	
	12042SMS3 Chassis	£1107.10s.
	English Electric Body 60 seats	£838.00d.
		£1945.10s.
August 9th	Trolley Bus No. 1 R.V. 4649	
	A.E.C. Chassis 4 wheeler No. 661T028	£1024.10s.
	English Electric Body	£785.00d.
		£1809.10s
	No. 3 R.V. 4651	
	A.E.C. Chassis No. 4 wheeler 661T030	£1024.10s.
	English Electric Body	£785.00s.
		£1909.10s.
August 11th	Trolley Bus. No. 9 R.V. 4657	
	Karrier Chassis No. 55004/ 4 wheeler	£1023.8s.9d
	English Electric Body 50 seater	£785.00.0d.
		£1808.8s.9d.
August 12th	Trolley Bus No. 12 R.V. 4658	
	A.E.C. 6 wheel chassis No. 663T074	£1230.00d.
	English Electric Body	£838.00d.
		£2068.00d.
August 15th	Trolley Bus No. 4 R.V. 4652	
	A.E.C. 4 wheeler Chassis No. 661T031	£1024.10s.
	English Electric Body	£785.00
		£1809.10s.
August 15th	Trolley Bus No. 8 R.V. 4656 4 wheeler	
	Sunbeam Chassis No 1300 4s	£994.10s.
	English Electric Body	£785.00s.
		£1779.10s

August 15th	Trolley Bus No. 2 R.V. 4650	
	A.E.C. Chassis No. 661T029	£1024.10s
	English Electric Body	£785.00s
		£1809.10s.

In February, 1934, work commenced on erecting the overhead equipment for the initial service from Cosham to South Parade Pier, at a cost of £8,238. The contractor was Clough, Smith and Co., Ltd., of London.

The first job was to erect additional poles at Portsbridge to support the weight of the trolley wires. In many instances, original tram poles were used but some were strengthened by pouring concrete inside them. While fixing the trolley wires, work was carried out to improve the street lighting. Every alternate pole was lengthened by cutting off 4 feet of the original pole then adding a tube 8 feet long. Construction of a turning circle at South Parade Pier started, and the overhead wires at Cosham compound were installed to take trolleys.

At the same time, June 1934, it was decided to extend the system from South Parade Pier to the Guildhall via Festing Road, Albert Road, Victoria Road North, Bradford Road and then on to Alexandra Park, Stamshaw. A provisional order

Complex overhead wires were needed to separate the traffic at Hilsea, near the Southdown garage, with trolley buses going to Northern Parade, Copnor Road and London Road. *(The News, Portsmouth)*

From tram to motor bus with a trolley bus inbetween. This unusual photograph of the three forms of Corporation transport was taken at Cosham compound. *(C.P.P.T.D.)*

Trolley bus Number 11 being given a tilt test before delivery. This vehicle was described by one driver as "a pig to drive". (C. Phillips)

Pictured before delivery, trolley bus fleet Number 15 was renumbered later as 215. (J. Dorey)

was made to extend from Alexandra Park along the new Northern Parade joining the existing system at Hilsea. It was also proposed that trolley buses should run along Northern Road to the foot of Portsdown Hill, the turning circle being round the Red Lion public house and into Spur Road.

On July 10, the first trolley bus was towed to Portsmouth and used for driver-training shortly afterwards. After examination by the Ministry of Transport on August 1, the first public service designated route, 3/4, left Cosham compound at 9.05 a.m. on August 4, 1934. A ten-minute frequency was maintained all day using seven trolley buses, fleet numbers 5, 6, 7, 10, 11, 14 and 15.

During the August Bank Holiday of 1934, 103 tramcars, 90 buses and seven trolley buses operated a two-minute service on the popular holiday routes, including Cosham for Portsdown Hill.

From August, 1934, to November, 1936, there was further activity in erecting new wires for the trolley bus system with additional poles where necessary to support the extra weight. At the same time the tram wire was removed. Special brackets were fixed to buildings to support the wires, the Corporation paying a nominal rent to the owners of the property.

In October, 1934, permission was sought to run trolley buses along the following routes: 1) Northern Parade, Northern Road to Cosham Red Lion; 2) Cosham High Street, Havant Road to Rectory Avenue, Farlington; 3) Northern Road to the Southampton Road boundary near Portchester; 4) Northern Road to the city boundary at the top of Portsdown Hill at Widley. The only one that was proceeded with was the first proposal, giving a full circle service, Cosham to Cosham.

After a five-month test period, Mr. Hall presented a report to the committee on the results of the tests of the 15 experimental trolley buses. The report gave details of the type of equipment used, average current consumption, acceleration and the time taken to reach 20 m.p.h., varying from 10 to 17 seconds. The quality of ride was considered, no doubt a necessity following the complaints about the tramcars.

The A.E.C. chassis with English Electric electrical equipment was described as good when laden but lively in the upper saloon when empty. The Karriers were said to be rather harsh. The Leyland Motors chassis with G.E.C. equipment did not do too well as the current consumption was rather high, acceleration was not so good and starting was jerky.

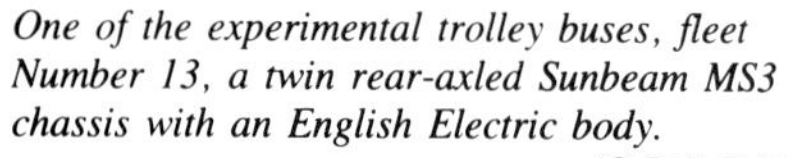

One of the experimental trolley buses, fleet Number 13, a twin rear-axled Sunbeam MS3 chassis with an English Electric body. (C.P.P.T.D.)

Trolley buses continued the patriotic tradition of being decorated for Royal events. Health and National Prosperity was proclaimed for the Coronation of George VI and Queen Elizabeth. (C.P.P.T.D.)

In September, 1935, Mr. Hall submitted a further report on the performance of the trial trolley buses with his recommendation for the purchase of nine with the A.E.C. chassis, English Electric electrical equipment and English Electric bodies. These were the cheapest to operate at 2.715d per mile.

Mr. Hall had stated that the "new medium", the trolley bus, had been so well received by the public that further extensions should be made, consequently, further trolley buses — fleet numbers 16 - 24 were ordered. Before its delivery, one of the batch was displayed at the 1935 Show at Olympia and number 20 was loaned to Brighton Corporation during December, 1935. Again it was necessary to borrow money for the expansion — £36,000 for the trolley buses and £18,000 for equipment.

Such was the success of the trolley bus, it was decided to complete the changeover from trams to trolley buses, with the result that the largest single order ever given for vehicles was placed. Cravens bodies were selected as it was the only manufacturer which could ensure delivery of a further 76 trolley buses.

The first to arrive was trolley bus fleet number 25 at 3.45 p.m. on July 17. Its registration number was R.V. 8307, chassis number 661T090 with a 52-passenger complement for its Craven body and chassis by English Electric Company (A.E.C.). The price of the chassis was £1,051 and body, £780. By November 10, 1936, a total of 52 were delivered and the remaining 24 arrived before January 20, 1937.

They all arrived with the department's new name in transfers on the nearside lower panel. From June 16, 1936, Portsmouth Corporation Tramways became City of Portsmouth Passenger Transport Department.

It was reported to the Tramways Committee in March, 1935, that the new trolley buses would not pass under the bridge at the town station, no doubt causing some embarrassment to Mr. Hall. The roadway under the bridge on the west side had been loweredin 1901 to take the trams. It was necessary, now, to lower the east side of the roadway to give a clearance of 17 feet, as the trolley buses were 15 feet 9 inches high and the original archway clearance was 16 feet 6 inches. The nine-inch clearance was insufficient to take the throughs and booms of the trolleys.

Throughout 1935 and well into 1936, the erection of poles and modifications to existing ones continued, at the same time many of the tram wires were removed. The overhead systems at Fratton Bridge were regarded as one of the most complicated in the country. The lines had the ability to link Fratton Bridge with Goldsmith Avenue or Bradford Junction and Fawcett Road. The weight of the wire was such that the trolley pole had to be fixed in the ground at an angle.

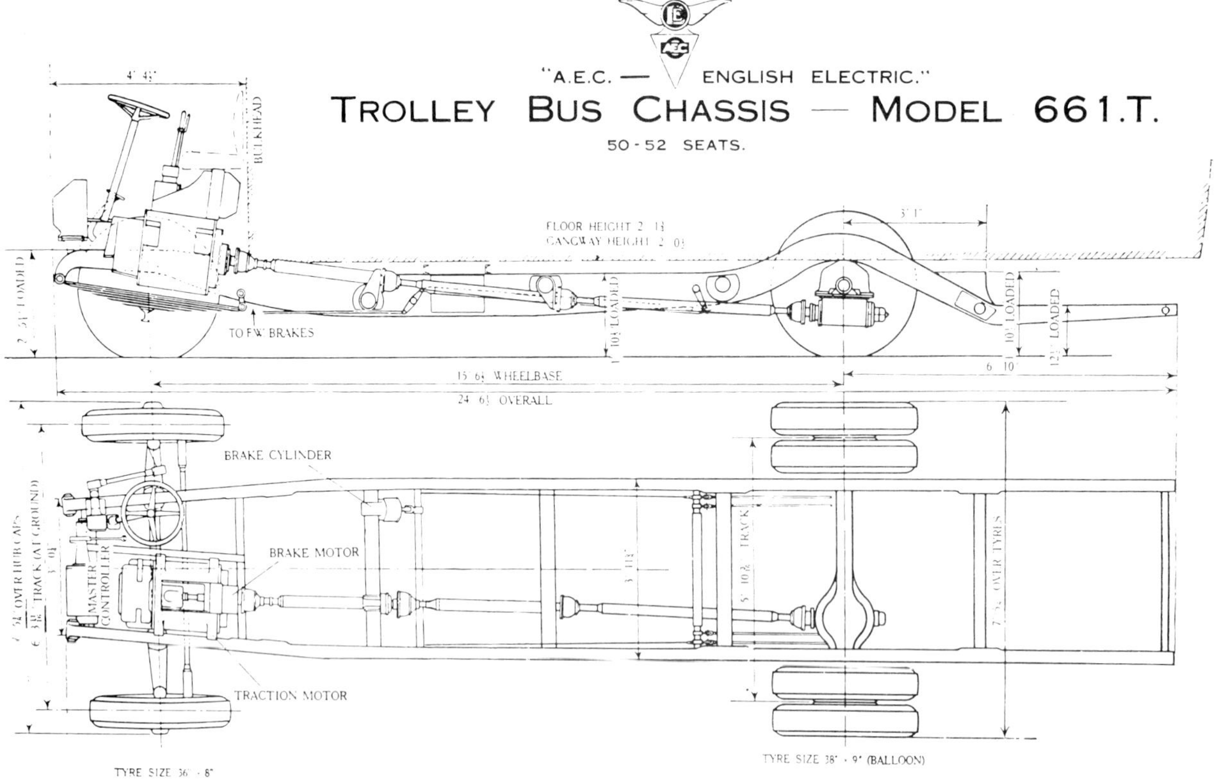

Arrangement of Chassis giving leading dimensions and positions of main units.
The current blue print of this Chassis should be applied for before putting bodywork in hand.

In February, 1936, it was announced that a new turning point for trolley buses was to be constructed as part of a £70,000 scheme to improve the esplanade at South Parade Pier. An extravagant scheme for the Lumps Fort and Canoe Lake area had been proposed, with details and a photograph of the model in the *Evening News*. The turning circle was completed a year later.

Extensive work was carried out at Hilsea constructing a series of traffic islands, during November. Because of the overhead wires, the trolleys had to have a special way made through the roadworks against the temporary flow of traffic. Needless to say, letters were sent to the *Evening News*, giving a variety of advice to the council. At the same time, work was going on at Kingston Cross installing a set of recently-introduced traffic signals, the first in Portsmouth. This caused many problems, due to the lack of experience of road users.

The trolley bus slowly was taking over from the tram. During 1934, 15 trolleys were in service, a further nine during 1935 and by August, 1936, 32. When the trams ceased in November, 1936, a total of 70 trolley buses were in service. On public holidays, 99 out of 100 were used.

Portsmouth was host to the annual conference of the Municipal Tramways and Transport Association in June, 1937. Mr. Hall presented a paper on trolley vehicles, expounding their virtues.

The department lost one of its closest political friends when Sir John Timpson died on October 19, 1937. He had been Chairman of the committee from 1917. Councillor W. Pugsley was appointed his successor and remained in office until his death in 1942, seeing the department through the difficult period of the Second World War.

Numerous dewirements occurred with the trolleys. One major problem was thought to be drivers being confused because buses and trolley buses looked much the same from the rear, as some of the bodies were of the same manufacture. If trolley bus drivers thought that a motor bus was in front of them but it was really another trolley using the same overhead wire and tried to overtake it, they dewired, causing all sorts of problems.

When Mr. Humpidge became Chief Assistant Engineer in November, 1937, one of his first jobs was to re-number the trolley bus fleet by adding 2 or 20 in front of the existing fleet number, so 1 became 201. All buses then had fleet numbers up to 199 with the large fleet numbers on the rear panel. It was hoped that by this means trolley bus drivers would know whether they were following another trolley or a bus.

Trolley buses Numbers 204 and 205 wait for passengers at Cosham compound. They were originally numbered 4 and 5. (J. Dorey)

A problem that was to occur many times during their life and sound the death knell of the trolley system was major roadworks. One example was the removal of tramlines in New Road, Buckland. The replacement of trolleys by buses for the work in New Road went on from November, 1937, to May, 1938. In many instances, the entire width of the road was taken up during major roadworks. Unfortunately, the inflexibility of the trolley bus was to work against it.

By the end of 1938, there were seven turning circles in use on the network — Cosham Red Lion, South Parade Pier, Cosham Railway Station, Clarence Pier, Milton, The Hard and Copnor Bridge. The only reverser was at Broad Street, Old Portsmouth. The total route mileage was 19.5 miles. Another turning circle, not wired for trolleys, was bought at the junction of Gladys Avenue and Northern Parade, Stamshaw, from United Breweries. The land had been used for allotments. During 1985, the site was sold by the Corporation for a flats development.

Electro or trolley

The public has always shown intense interest in its transport system: One correspondent to the *Evening News* suggested that trolley bus was the wrong term. He felt they should be called electro buses. The *Evening News* always missed out the "e", calling them "trolly" buses. The newspaper did report the first trolley bus being towed through Southampton and stated that the people there looked on enviously. By July 19, it was reporting that a trolley bus had been seen running between Cosham and North End for the last three or four mornings on driver training.

Teething troubles

The introduction of the trolley was not without its problems. During the morning of August 15, a trolley bus over-ran its pole limit in London Road, Hilsea, and shorted the overhead wires. Some wires became detached and sparks flew from them, causing a horse to bolt. Many motorists and pedestrians kept well clear. The unfortunate incident stopped all trolley buses and trams and it was well over an hour before everything was back in working order. At one time, seven tramcars and six trolley buses were marooned.

The *Evening News* editorial had sympathy for the drivers, many had been tram drivers, who, as yet, were not fully experienced and they now had to steer. It was hoped that the drivers would regard motorists as a better race than they thought they were. It was felt that with more experience, such mishaps would decrease and everyone would be happy.

A Ministry of Transport official had watched the introduction of trolley buses carefully and declared that breakdowns had been fewer than he had expected.

First death

The office diary for December 12, 1934, records the first fatal accident involving a trolley bus. A Marine pensioner, Mr. Thomas Temple, was said to have walked across the road in front of the trolley bus. A verdict of Accidental death was recorded and the driver exonerated from all blame. The diary records three fatal accidents for 1934, again showing the poor level of awareness of all road users. The trolley bus was very quiet in operation and this, no doubt, did not help to warn pedestrians of its presence.

Touchy subject

Over the years, there have been numerous minor complaints, usually started by a letter to the Editor of the *Evening News*. One item that created some interest was fleas. Numerous people wrote to the department and the newspaper complaining about dogs being allowed to travel on buses and sit on seats. Most seats were the upholstered type with springs stuffed with horsehair and covered in moquette, an ideal home for fleas.

One woman challenged a fellow passenger as to why his dog was scratching. "He's only got fleas," was the reply. There followed the usual for and against correspondence about dogs. The charge was full fare for dogs of a size to be carried on the lap of a passenger, at the discretion of the conductor. This brought a Mr. Green, of Duke Street, into court on February 5, 1935. He was summonsed to appear for allowing his dog to occupy a seat. When the conductor challenged him, Mr. Green used insulting remarks. He was fined £1 with 7s6d (37½p) costs.

CHAPTER VIII

TROLLEYS AT WAR

During the summer of 1939, war clouds were gathering over Europe but an extensive schedule of services was organised for the season.

These were:

Route 1 Cosham Red Lion, North End, Guildhall, Clarence Pier;
Route 2 Reverse of Route 1;
(Six vehicles were used to give a ten-minute frequency.)
Route 3A Cosham railway, North End, Fratton Bridge, Fawcett Road, South Parade Pier;
Route 4A, Reverse of 3A;
Route 3 South Parade Pier, Albert Road, Bradford Junction, Guildhall, Alexandra Park, Cosham Red Lion;
Route 4, Reverse of 3;
(Six vehicles for ten-minute frequency.)
Route 5 Dockyard, Palmerston Road, South Parade Pier, Eastney, Milton, White House, Fratton Bridge, Guildhall (to Dockyard as required);
Route 6, Reverse of 5;
(Eight vehicles, ten-minute frequency.)
Route 11 Copnor Bridge, Lake Road, Guildhall, Dockyard;
Route 12, Reverse of 11;
(Four vehicles, ten-minute frequency.)
Route 15 Copnor Bridge, Lake Road, Guildhall, Floating Bridge, Old Portsmouth;
Route 16, Reverse of 15;
(Four vehicles, ten-minute frequency.)
Route 17 Dockyard, Guildhall, Albert Road, Eastney, Milton, White House, Guildhall, Dockyard;
Route 18, Reverse of 17;
(Nine vehicles, ten-minute frequency.)

These proposals for the summer service were maintained until September when a further re-organisation took place. This was to release motor buses from service to be used for transporting children to the railway station for evacuation.

At the outbreak of war, all trolley buses and buses had their roofs painted grey. The front edge of the front mudguards, lifeguards and the entrance step were painted white. Headlamps were fitted with masks to reduce the light emitted from them.

Mr. Hall experimented with a blue lacquer painted on all windows to reduce glare but this was expensive and not very effective. Dipping light bulbs in the lacquer proved cheaper and more successful. Later in the war Mr. Hall developed a spark shield to fit over the frogs and crossings to prevent the sparks being seen by enemy pilots. It is believed he did this after the blitz on Sheffield where there was a theory that German bomber pilots had seen the sparks from tram wires and followed them to the city centre.

A similar problem occurred in the Guildhall Square when trolley buses were turning round and the conductors disconnected the overhead trolley poles. They had to use torches at night to find the overhead wire to re-connect and their action was described as a mini-searchlight display. The problem was overcome by installing a turning circle.

In November, 1939, there was a proposal to make Twyford Avenue northbound and Stamshaw Road southbound, as it is today. The alteration would have created problems and considerable cost to the department in fixing new overhead equipment. The proposal was shelved for the duration of the war, as the Ministry of Transport would not consider any one-way systems unless they had an advantageous affect on the war effort.

By order of the War Office, no buses were allowed to show their destination if they referred to Government establishments such as the Dockyard. A notice appeared in the *Evening News* stating these alterations; all the spies needed to know was that the 17/18 service and others went to the Dockyard.

The head office at Eastney was sandbagged and shutters fitted, and the roof of the office was used as a fire watch post. Mr. Hall had a bath fitted in the office as he spent many nights there. A single bed he used was found recently in the loft at the office.

From July, 1940, the seafront area was put out of bounds to buses. Services using the Clarence Pier and South Parade Pier turning circles were stopped short at the Pier Hotel, now Rees Hall, Bellevue Terrace. Later in the war, before the D-Day preparations, the public was kept from the seafront and some of the wire was temporarily removed at the request of the Government.

In July, 1940, an air raid, the first to affect the trolley bus system, caused damage in Old Portsmouth. On August 24, a direct hit on the Princes Theatre in Lake Road, Landport, caused extensive damage to the overhead wires.

Trolley buses — fleet numbers 201 - 224 — had not been fitted with batteries when they were built, consequently, when the alterations to terminal points and damage to overhead wires occurred, these vehicles were stranded, creating many difficulties for the engineering staff. After the air raids, the problem had become so great that it was decided to lay up all these vehicles on waste ground off Northern Parade, Hilsea, for the duration of the war. The remainder of the trolley buses had the ability to travel about six miles on their batteries, at walking pace.

A number of trolley buses and motor buses were loaned to other authorities during the Second World War, including trolley bus 215, pictured in Pontypridd, Wales. (J. Dorey)

The four six-wheeler trolleys also were surplus to requirements. Nottingham City Transport tried to buy them but negotiations broke down at the last minute. Later, they were loaned to Pontypridd Urban District Council and during 1942 they were towed to Wales. Numbers 212 and 215 returned in October, 1945, and 213 and 214 came back in March, 1945. Number 212 was never used in service again. The others were returned to use after major work on them in 1947 and 1949.

During the worst air raid of the war experienced by Portsmouth in January, 1941, a direct hit on the power station stranded trolley buses all over the city, seriously affecting many routes. It is believed a temporary supply of power was obtained from the Dockyard.

During another air raid in March, 1941, extensive damage was inflicted on Commercial Road and Lake Road. The damage was such that the overhead wire for High Street was not reinstated until July, 1941, single-decker buses providing a service into Old Portsmouth and the Floating Bridge.

Mr. Hall's report to a special committee stated: "The air raid on the night of the 10/11 March commenced at 7.50 p.m., answered by a continuous barrage of fire from the ground. At approximately 8.50 p.m., the electricity supply to the city was completely cut off, every trolley bus was rendered immobile. All the crews stood by their vehicles until they were returned to their respective depots."

At about 1.50 a.m., three high explosive bombs fell on Eastney Depot and exploded after falling through the roof and hitting one of the main girders in the east bay of the-then bus section. Fire destroyed some of the stores and slight water damage was done to machinery. Ten buses were destroyed completely — four double-deckers, five single-deckers and one of the seafront runabouts. Three of the single-deckers were Leyland Cheetah type, delivered just before the war. The estimated cost of the damage was £30,000 to £40,000.

The foreman on duty was praised for removing several vehicles away from the fire to a safe place. A number of vehicles parked in the garage and streets around the depot had superficial damage, generally broken windows. Mr. Hall's report on the raid described the city as being in a state of confusion. The entire trolley bus system was shut down. A limited amount of power was available from about 2 p.m. on Thursday, March 13, when it was possible to operate 15 trolley buses only.

On the morning of March 11, a number of drivers failed to report for work; some had been on fire watch duty all night and 25 men lost their homes. Only a skeleton service could be operated. The first priority was workmen's services, although police closed many major roads. As some routes were re-opened, they were closed again almost immediately when unexploded bombs were found. The greatest difficulty was at Portsbridge where an unexploded bomb on the bridge meant that the only way into Portsmouth was over the temporary bridge across Port Creek to the east of Portsbridge. A total of 61 buses, about half the fleet, was allocated to various services with 13 used for evacuating people from the city and three detailed for police requirements.

North End depot suffered bomb damage during the same air raid but no vehicles were damaged. The roof in the centre section, previously all glass and painted black at the start of the war, was eventually replaced with metal sheets.

Royal Marines from Eastney Barracks were made available to help clear debris and make temporary repairs at Eastney Depot. Mr. Hall praised all the staff of the department but, with regret, he reported the death of a trolley bus driver who was killed on his way home during the air raid.

During these difficult times, the Corporation was running services to Waterlooville and Cowplain, duplicating the Southdown routes. It was reported that many people were leaving the south of the city to move inland away from the air raids.

To conserve diesel oil, every possible use was made of the trolley bus, as the country was self-sufficient in coal to produce the electricity. After a conference in Reading of transport operators, the Regional Transport Commissioner insisted on a reduction in operations. From January, 1943, late night services were curtailed, with all last departures from the city at 9 p.m.

Throughout the war, many problems were overcome by the Transport Department, such as damage to roads and overhead equipment. The availability of spares was overcome in many cases by making spares in the workshops. There is still a lathe in the workshop in everyday use stamped "war finish".

North End depot suffered in the Second World War from an air raid which damaged its roof. This photograph was taken in 1902 soon after it was built. *(T.H. Dethridge)*

Woman at the wheel

Mrs. Vicky Hathaway, now Mrs. Webb, aged 80, and living at Lee-on-Solent, was recruited as a driver in 1941. When she moved to Portsmouth from Reading, an inspector heard that she had driven lorries so offered her a job and arranged an immediate Public Service Vehicle driving test in a Dennis single-decker. She passed on a route which included North End and Fratton Road, then on May 21, 1942, she gained an all groups P.S.V. licence to drive double-deckers.

During air raids, drivers were instructed to take passengers to the nearest air raid shelter and ensure their safety. A working day usually started at 6 a.m. carrying men and women to the Dockyard. After several breaks during the day she often volunteered to drive the bus that took pensioners late at night to the air raid shelters under Portsdown Hill. Mrs. Webb recalled the sadness and degradation that the air raids had brought to people. The passengers had not been able to bath themselves or wash their clothes because of the loss of water supply following air raids.

During one raid she drove a single-decker to the nearest shelter while shrapnel rained on the roof of the bus.

On another occasion, driving her bus to the Dockyard along Chichester Road, North End, she stopped where a house had received a direct hit with a land mine. Mrs. Webb recognised a woman doctor who was carrying what appeared to be a bundle of rags. The doctor passed the bundle to Mrs. Webb, telling her to take the baby to hospital immediately. As quickly as possible, she made an unscheduled detour to the Royal Hospital but, unfortunately, the baby died.

There were happier times when the drivers and conductors organised a concert party, which sang to the injured soldiers at Queen Alexandra Hospital, including Mrs. Webb as Salome. Three separate victory celebration dinners were held in May, 1946, to ensure that all employees of the department had an opportunity to attend.

Act of kindness

Mr. Bill Jones, who was bodyshop foreman for many years until his retirement in 1976 worked in the depot at the time of the March, 1941, air raid. He tells of the morning after the raid when he met Mr. Hall, who inquired if he had any problems. Unfortunately, Bill's house had been damaged so Mr. Hall sent him home on three day's leave to sort out his numerous difficulties. After 40 years, Bill still remembers that act of kindness by Mr. Hall, who was respected by all.

CHAPTER IX

BUSES AT WAR

The office diary is one of the main sources of information for this book as there are regular entries from January 1, 1901, to September 3, 1939. The entry for that final day is: " Outbreak of war with Germany." The only wartime entry is in October, 1940: "Penny fare abolished, 1½d adult minimum."

During the first two days of September, 1939, buses were requisitioned for the evacuation of the civilian population of Portsmouth. Two *Evening News* photographs show a fleet of double-deckers bringing children from districts of the city to the town station yard for transport on to safer areas.

In October, 1940, the Regional Transport Commissioner requested that ten double-decker vehicles be loaned to the London Passenger Transport Board. Public transport had been disrupted considerably in London by the air raids and a massive influx of Service people into the capital. London required over 2,000 additional buses. The ten petrol-engined Tilling Stevens, which had been unlicensed in the depot for some time before the war, were sent to London on October 24, returning to Portsmouth in March 1941, to be loaned out again to Southampton and the Hants and Sussex Coach Company. The charge to London was £25 a month for each vehicle hired.

Corporation buses collected children from throughout the city to assemble at Portsmouth and Southsea railway station ready for evacuation on September 3, 1939.
(The News, Portsmouth)

One of the Portsmouth buses which was loaned to London Transport during the Second World War was fleet Number 80, a Tilling Stevens. *(C.P.P.T.D.)*

These details were recorded by Mr. Hall in February, 1941, in notes to the Transport Committee, following the air raid on Portsmouth in January, 1941. Mr. Hall was concerned that there could be a loss of vehicles in any future raid. A month later, his fears were realised when Eastney depot was damaged and ten buses destroyed. One of these was the only A.E.C. Regent in the fleet, number 35, originally bought in 1931. The engine and gearbox were salvaged and sold to Nottingham City Transport.

The war was to give Mr. Hall the opportunity to expand services beyond the Red Lion at Cosham as large numbers of people had moved out of Portsmouth to Waterlooville and Cowplain to escape the air raids.

The Regional Transport Commissioner called a conference between the Corporation and Southdown. Numerous complaints had been received from residents about the poor service beyond Cosham to Cowplain and Southdown was unable to cope with the extra passengers at peak periods. The commissioner made it quite clear that he was aware of the problem and that augmentation of the service in certain directions was required. He said that the Corporation was the right authority to provide the additional vehicles as it had lost passengers in the city. The Corporation did provide services to Waterlooville and occasionally on to Cowplain but it was one-way traffic. In the morning the buses travelled to Waterlooville empty, known in the trade as dead mileage, then they brought people into the city. At the evening peak, the situation was reversed. An interim agreement was made with Southdown and the Corporation was not allowed to carry passengers in both directions.

The massive increase in the price of fuel oil and tyres during the early part of the war and the loss of passengers created a potential financial problem. Fares were allowed to increase by one halfpenny, which was estimated to produce an extra £40,000 revenue.

North End depot did not escape damage in raids, the roof of the original tramway paintshop received a direct hit from a bomb. After the trams had been disposed of this part of the depot had not been used. Consequently, repairs to the roof were not completed until 1949.

The supply of new buses during the war was severely restricted as most of the factories had been utilised for the manufacture of military machines. The Charles Roe factory in Leeds, for example, was reorganised to make tanks. The whole production of Leylands was turned over to war equipment. A type of bus engine from Leylands was used in tanks and in the post-war years these were fitted to the Leyland P.D.1.

Portsmouth was able to obtain new buses from 1942-44 in part to replace those that had been lost during the air raid. Ten Bedford O.W.B.s were delivered during 1942-3, eight had bodies by Duple and the others by Mulliner. They were almost identical as they were built to the Ministry of Supply's spartan specifications. Nine double-decker Daimler C.W.A.6 models arrived in 1944 with bodies by Duple, a spartan finish and those dreaded wooden slat seats. The bodies on the Daimlers did not last long, as in less than ten years they were rebodied by Crossleys, of Manchester. Engineering staff removed the bodies from the chassis of the Daimlers, the chassis were then stripped completely and all the parts were overhauled and reassembled.

The Bedford O.W.B.s were based at Southdown's Hayling Island garage when they operated on Southdown routes. They were used to "run off" mileage "owed" by the Corporation to Southdown under the joint agreement. They were lightweight vehicles and proved useful operating over the old bridge to Hayling as heavier buses owned by Southdown were not allowed on the bridge. The Bedfords could not cross with a full load of passengers either. On many occasions, male passengers had to get off and walk across the bridge, rejoining the bus on the other side.

One of the Bedfords, found in a field in Cornwall, has been preserved. It was brought to Bishop's Waltham and stood in the open for several years until it was bought by Cliff Burgess, a member of a vintage transport association. Portsmouth City Museums has provided covered accommodation for the restoration and, hopefully, it will not be too long before C.T.P. 200 fleet number 170 is running again.

The hardship of wartime was experienced by all members of the staff who remained with the department throughout the war. As in many industries, it was commonplace to work a 12-hour shift on their ordinary job and then report for fire-watch duties. The author found an internal memorandum from Mr. Hall to one of the engineering staff, Mr. Barratt: "The Medical Officer confirms that you are now fit to continue your normal duties and fire-watch duties." The memorandum was in an old clock card rack that had been removed from North End depot. Mr. Barratt may well have received a reprimand for disobeying instruction because he never received the memo.

About 50 employees were trained in fire-fighting and 30 of these were lectured on the effects of gas attacks. It was expected that the buses would continue running

Bus Number 170, pictured on a Cosham route, was a Bedford OWB with a wartime utility body. It entered service in 1944 and was used for the first post-war one-man operation. It was withdrawn by 1963.

Shortages of many materials led to the imposition of utility standards for the few buses which were produced during the war. Fleet Number 175, built in 1944, had a Daimler C.W.A.6. wartime chassis with a utility body by Mulliner.

Many of the utility bodies were replaced later. Fleet Number 173, with a Daimler C.W.A.6. chassis, was rebodied in 1955 by Crossley.
(J. Dorey)

After 20 years in Cornwall, bus Number 170 was found by Mr. C. Burgess (pictured second from right) and is now being completely restored to its former state.
(C. Burgess)

after any gas attack. Instructions were given for buses to carry on after any air raid warning until they heard the sound of aircraft or gunfire.

The Auxillary Fire Service had fire engines at North End and Eastney depots, the A.F.S. men being provided with crew facilities. The fire hoses and stand-pipe issued during the war are still in the stores at Eastney and were checked for action during the strike by the fire brigade in 1979. Many innovative ideas were tried to improve vehicles' performance and save fuel, including the conversion of five buses in June, 1943, to run on gas. None of the men involved with these vehicles thought the gas producers towed behind buses were successful. One of the problems was that the gas was very dirty and blocked the jets of the carburettor. The gas producers were abandoned in December, 1944.

As in the First World War, a large proportion of men were called up for wartime service and, again, women were recruited. Out of a total of 583 women employed, 490 were platform staff. Portsmouth claims to have had the first woman to qualify as a public service vehicle driver.

There were ordinary accidents, too, in the war. Fleet Number 101 came to grief on the greasy surface of Tangier Road, Copnor.
(C.P.P.T.D.)

Women were recruited in large numbers during the war, mainly as conductresses, to free men for the Services. Senior officers are pictured with some of the conductresses.
(C.P.P.T.D.)

The war memorial at the Highland Road office with the names of department men killed in both world wars. The lower half of the memorial was made by Bill Jones, the former bodyshop foreman, and the brass coat of arms was made by his father. (C.P.P.T.D.)

A Leyland TD1 in the Guildhall Square passes a department kiosk made from timber salvaged from the roof of North End depot which was damaged in an air raid. (J. Dorey)

Forty years later the kiosk has withstood the rigours of time to become an outdoor toy store for a play school at Milton. (Author)

Good out of bad

Some good did come out of the air raid which damaged the roof of North End depot in March, 1941. The timber, which was very scarce, was salvaged and used to build a kiosk for the Guildhall Square in January, 1943. The clock above the kiosk was presented to the city by the company which supplied all the clocks to the Transport Department for bus shelters. The kiosk is now used as a toy store at a children's centre at Milton and the mechanism from the clock was fitted to one of the clocks on top of the changing rooms at Farlington playing fields or the King George V Playing Fields, Cosham.

Goodwill punctured

Reg Thorpe, now an active 80-year-old, spent the war working for the department. After years of driving lorries round the country, he joined the buses in 1936. He was involved in the evacuation of expectant mothers, taking them from Portsmouth to Abingdon, Berkshire. On one trip his bus had a double rear puncture and he could not go any further. He removed both wheels from the nearside rear and fitted a spare wheel then a passing lorry took him to Newbury where he was allowed to repair both flat tyres in a garage workshop. He was charged eight shillings (40p) for the use of equipment and patches. On his return to Portsmouth, he had difficulty in getting his money back as he was unable to produce a slip of paper as a receipt. When he was refused repayment, he had a few choice words to say to two rather difficult men in the office then he went to see the Traffic Superintendent and threatened to join up. It wasn't long before Reg had his eight shillings back.

On other occasions, he took a bus to Glasgow, Edinburgh and along the Kent coast. The Royal Navy had commandeered the bus and converted it to a mobile gunnery training school by taking out all the seats. The lower saloon was a classroom and the top deck was fitted with a gun for the trainees.

Slow going

Tony Bushell, now enjoying retirement after 34 years with the department, tells of when he delivered bus chassis for rebodying to Crossley's of Manchester. He made several journeys during the winter of 1954/55 on an open chassis at a maximum speed of 28 m.p.h. The journey took one and a half days. By the first night, he arrived at Ashbourne in Derbyshire where he had bed and breakfast with the local vicar. When the first chassis had been rebodied, he was able to start his return journey at lunchtime on the second day. On one occasion when he was returning to Portsmouth with two others, the late George West and the late Sid Fryatt, they were stopped by police at Harwell, near Oxford, as the A34 was blocked completely by snow. They turned the buses round and stayed two nights in Oxford until the roads were cleared.

CHAPTER X

DECLINE OF THE TROLLEYS

In early May, 1946, trolley bus number 204 was decorated for Safety Week and several vehicles were festooned with "G.R." and crowns as part of the victory celebrations later in the month. Trolley buses 201 to 211 were returned to service after semi-retirement on waste ground off Northern Parade for most of the war.

Many of the employees were returning from the Forces to their peace-time work; there was a need to plan and look forward to the future, bearing in mind the problems of the war.

The first trolley bus service to be replaced by buses was the then 1 and 2 service as M/N, being extended to Rectory Avenue, Farlington, from May 18, 1947. It was intended to be a temporary arrangement as plans were being made to extend trolley bus routes.

Seven routes were planned: Cosham Red Lion to Drayton and Farlington; Milton White House to the Coach and Horses, Hilsea, via Copnor Road; North End and Gladys Avenue to Alexandra Park; Stubbington Avenue, North End, to Copnor Road; Copnor Bridge to Tangier Road and Stanley Avenue; Commercial Road and Edinburgh Road to Unicorn Road; Spur Road, Cosham, to Wymering, Paulsgrove and Portchester crossroads.

The city celebrated the end of the Second World War in style. Trolley bus Number 204 was flamboyantly decorated for the victory celebrations. *(H. Draper)*

Again, for the accession of Queen Elizabeth vehicles were decorated with symbols and lights. This shield, used on a trolley bus, is now in storage at Eastney. *(Author)*

The proposed extensions were to expand the system to areas such as the developing Paulsgrove estate. The alterations would also give a through service from outlying areas to central Portsmouth, in many instances eliminating waiting at several terminal points and removing the need for passengers to change from bus to trolley bus at Cosham. The only option taken up was to run a trolley system along Copnor Road from the White House at Milton to the Coach and Horses, Hilsea. A link between London Road and Copnor Road, along Chichester Road, was made later.

During the period between the end of the war to the mid-1950s, the future of the trolley bus system was discussed at great length. There were considerable debates by the Transport Committee and the public through the Press. There is no doubt that the trolley buses had given a good service but the need of the city to expand and rehouse the people of Portsmouth at Leigh Park had to be considered.

The proposed extensions to Paulsgrove and the one along Havant Road to Rectory Avenue were to prove too expensive. Up to the joint agreement with Southdown, the Transport Department operations had been confined to the area south of Cosham railway gates. The proposals were costed at £7,500 a mile. A small saving was made by buying secondhand poles from London Transport for the Copnor Road and Chichester Road extensions. The installation was undertaken by the department's own staff in 1952, under the direction of Charles Phillips.

Trolley bus fleet Number 312 with a Burlingham body was new in 1951. The poster in the front window advertises services to and from the circus at Southsea. *(G.H Truran)*

There were many day-to-day problems to overcome. In October, 1947, both booms came off one trolley bus and caused a short circuit at peak time with the section between Fratton Bridge and Lake Road dead from 4 p.m. to 5.20 p.m. On another occasion, passengers missed the curtain up at the King's Theatre, Southsea, due to a power failure.

A frequent job for the overhead linesman was to change the carbon slippers at the end of the trolley boom. Years before, the original wheels were replaced with a slipper to reduce wear on the overhead wire. In dry weather, the slippers were very successful but when it rained there were serious problems as the water combined with carbon dust to make a grinding paste. It was a common occurrence to fit new slippers at South Parade Pier and change them again at the Red Lion at Cosham. This could be done from the top deck rear emergency window.

After much debate, it was decided to buy new trolley buses — 15 Burlingham bodied B.U.T. vehicles, the chassis costing £2,371 and the bodies £2,280. The first four were in service by November, 1950.

There were three rows of overhead wire at the Dockyard gates on The Hard, Portsea, to accommodate the number of trolley buses using the terminus. Bus stop plates at that time gave detailed information. *(L. Bern)*

January, 1951, marked the fiftieth anniversary of the department and the retirement of Mr. Ben Hall. Both occasions were marked by a civic banquet. During his 25 years' service, Mr. Hall had seen considerable change. When he joined the department, there were 34 buses and 116 trams; at his retirement, there were 115 buses and 100 trolley buses.

In March, 1951, the new General Manager, Mr. H.C. Simmonds reviewed his fleet which consisted of 31 buses over 15 years old and 49 buses between ten and 15 years old. His plan was to replace 25 in 1951/2 and 25 in each of the following two years. The trolley buses were at least 12 years old and a minimum requirement in the next ten years would be to replace ten every year. Many of the original trolley buses were delicensed and had not been used for many years.

With the need to carry out repairs to the overhead system on a regular basis, two Leyland TD 2 buses were converted to tower wagons. The original bus body was removed, the chassis shortened and a folding tower fitted to both. Fortunately, both these vehicles are preserved, T.W.1 owned by the City Museums and T.W.2 preserved in a a private collection by a former Portsmouth resident, Mr. John Dorey.

Mr. Ben Hall, General Manager from 1926 to 1951, oversaw a period of tremendous change and development in the department, encompassing the decline of the tram, the increasing use of motor buses, wartime difficulties, and the heyday of public transport.

The Transport Department mounted a display showing the scope of its workshops for an engineering exhibition held at Southsea Common in 1950. *(C.P.P.T.D.)*

Eastney depot workshops were self-sufficient for maintenance of most items. This photograph of the ticket machine repair shop was taken in 1951 to mark the 50th anniversary of the department. *(The News, Portsmouth)*

The engine repairs shop in 1951 where engines from Leyland T.D.4s were being overhauled before being fitted into Crossley buses. *(The News, Portsmouth)*

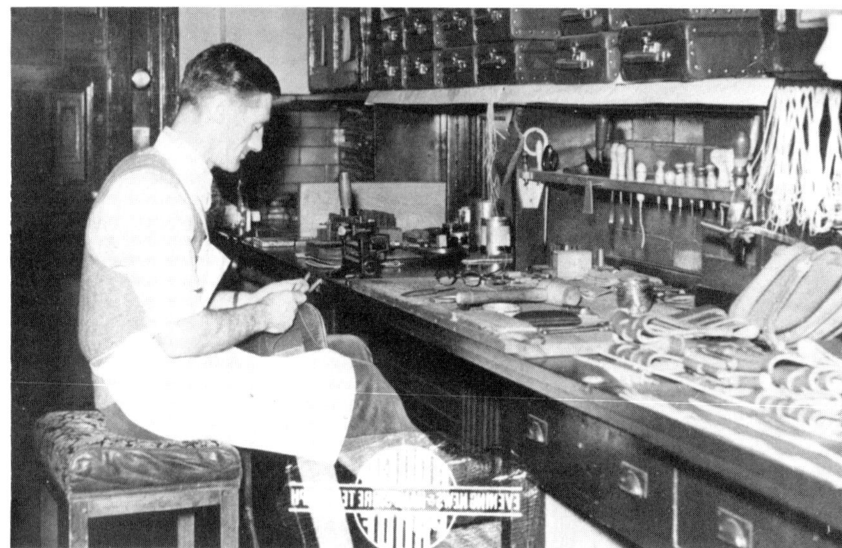

Conductor's cash bags and boxes were made and mended in the saddler's shop at Eastney. *(The News, Portsmouth)*

Tower wagon Number 1, T.W.1, was used for the installation and repair of overhead wires on the trolley bus system. It was converted from bus Number 17.

In September, 1951, the first section of overhead equipment was removed when the route to the Floating Bridge was abandoned. A correspondent to the *Evening News* commented that it had been removed so quickly he wondered if the equipment was to be used on the extension to Hilsea. This first abandonment of any part of the trolley system encouraged many people to protest and offer advice through the *Evening News*.

Another correspondent suggested that the overhead from the Floating Bridge be used to equip the turning circle at South Parade Pier. The length of overhead on Northern Road from Cosham compound to Portsbridge had been unused since the private road to Cosham compound had been wired for trolleys. There was also redundant overhead wire in Northern Parade and the wire in Rugby Road, Southsea, had been used rarely. It is said that the wire was as good on the day it was taken down as on the day it was erected.

The early 1950s saw the beginning of the end for the trolley bus. Mr. Simmonds's review of the state of the fleet highlighted the need to spend a considerable amount of money on refurbishing the bodies of the trolley buses. The complete front ends had to be rebuilt because the timber, which was kiln-dried, had rotted, a problem made worse by water retained in the framework behind aluminium panels.

In March, 1954, the Ratepayers Association asked that no further trolley bus routes be abandoned. Members were disturbed that the system was being allowed to decline. Ten trolley buses were sold in 1953 for £50 and a further 20 were in storage at Eastney depot. The public did not know it at the time but those in storage were not safe to be on the road.

Despite the signs of decline, a Walsall trolley bus ran on trial in the city for three weeks, partly during the Municipal Passenger Transport Association Conference of September 27 - 30.

Alderman H.E. Collins, the Chairman of the Transport Committee, had said in April, 1954, that trolley buses should be phased out over ten years but in March, 1956, there were rumours among staff that the system was going to close. Alderman Collins said he paid no attention to rumours, there was little difference between the cost of running buses and trolley buses. The problem was the need to expand beyond Cosham and the capital cost of the overhead equipment. The proposed one-way system for Twyford Avenue and Stamshaw Road was raised again but the cost of wiring would have been excessive.

Another conversion of a redundant bus was a lorry used for waste disposal. It was formerly bus Number 105, a Crossley Condor.

The Suez crisis in the Middle East, which seriously affected oil supplies, led to a two-hour debate in the city council of April, 1956, but no decision about the future of the trolley system was taken.

On July 30, 1956, the Transport Committee passed the following resolution: "That the policy of this committee is not to extend the trolley bus system but to authorise the General Manager gradually to reduce it and in the interests of economy and efficiency to replace it with motorbuses."

On its way to the Dockyard, trolley bus fleet Number 294, with an A.E.C. chassis and Craven body, turns into New Road at Copnor Bridge.

At that time, there were 21 unlicensed trolley buses waiting a decision by the committee on whether they should be rebuilt. There was, of course, criticism for spending money on the Copnor Road and Chichester Road system and calls for its abandonment. An 11-page report by the Ratepayers Association again put up the case for keeping the system, as it did not rely on imported oil. The Labour Party Delegates on the Council viewed the proposed abandonment with alarm.

In September, 1956, the committee again considered ending the trolley bus system which had an outstanding loan debt of £57,616 plus interest. The anticipated life of the overhead and vehicles was six to eight years. Duplication and extension of the system to 34 miles would cost £260,000.

The trolley bus system had a loss of £4,774 in the previous year, while the motor bus account had a profit of £22,193, although "it wasn't the type of vehicle that gives the profit or loss but the routes they run on," stated Alderman Collins.

The co-ordination agreement came in for criticism, as £11,000 of the Corporation receipts had been passed over to Southdown. Alderman Collins stated that in 1959 trolley buses had operated 200,000 miles more than in 1939 with 18 fewer vehicles. The object of the co-ordination agreement had been achieved and wasteful mileage had been reduced. Trolley buses were cheaper to operate until the cost of the overhead was considered. The Paulsgrove extension would have cost £38,000 plus 15 new trolley buses at £6,400 each.

In October, 1956, the city council upheld the decision of the Transport Committee. One councillor said that the glorified tramcar of 1934/5 was a luxury Portsmouth could not afford. To be economic, the Transport Department had to operate beyond Cosham to the new council estates.

But only three months later the Suez crisis created support for keeping the trolley bus. Both Southdown and the Corporation reduced evening bus services to save fuel while trolley buses stood waiting to be scrapped. In January, 1957, the city council voted by 27 votes to 24 to reconsider the plans to abandon the trolley buses. Alderman Collins quoted the amount of money that would be required and said the city would be committed to trolley bus operation for 20 years. One councillor

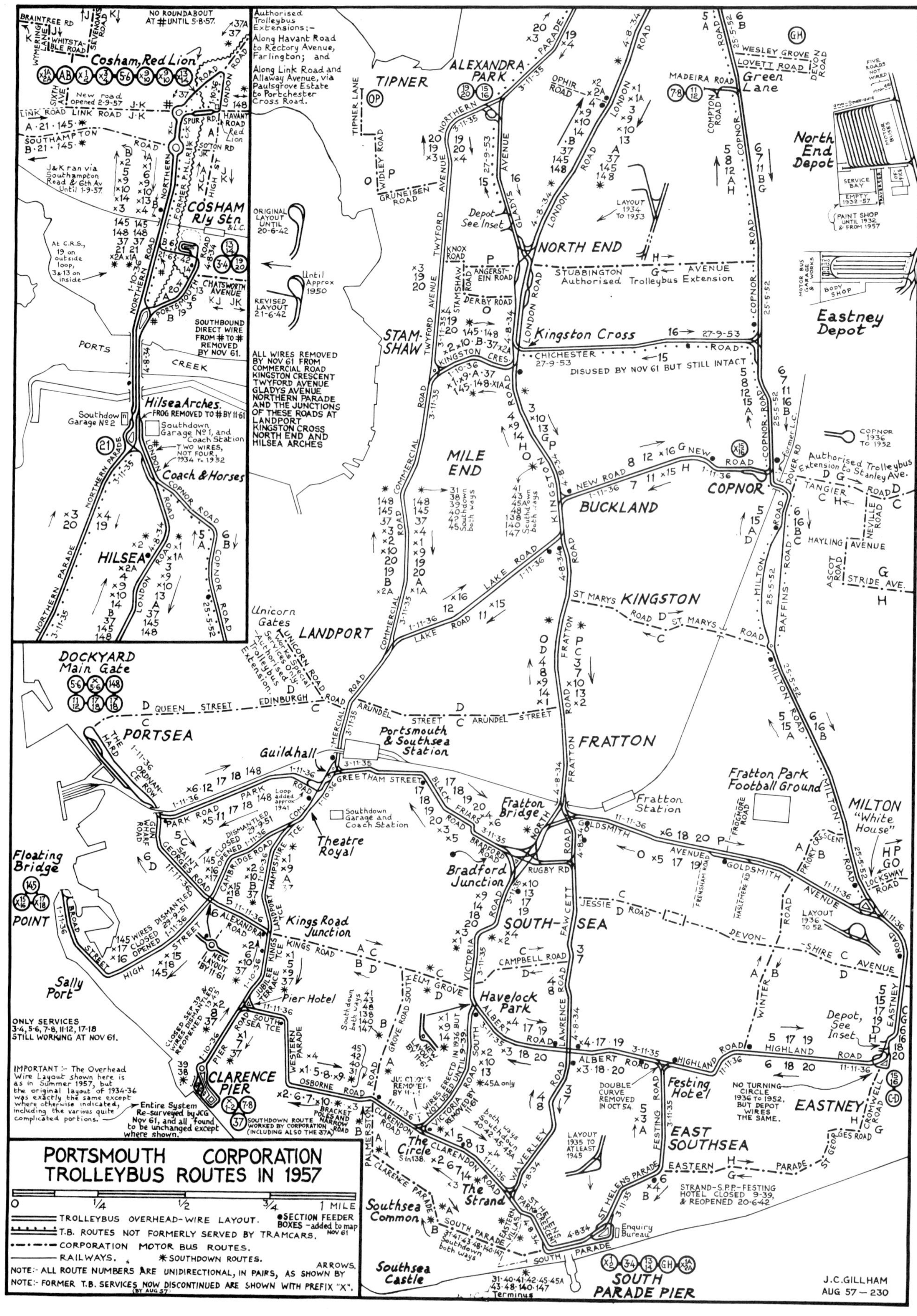
PORTSMOUTH CORPORATION
TROLLEYBUS ROUTES IN 1957
0
1/4
1/2
3/4
1 MILE
TROLLEYBUS OVERHEAD-WIRE LAYOUT.
T.B. ROUTES NOT FORMERLY SERVED BY TRAMCARS.
CORPORATION MOTOR BUS ROUTES.
RAILWAYS.
✱ SOUTHDOWN ROUTES.
●SECTION FEEDER BOXES - added to map Nov 61
NOTE:- ALL ROUTE NUMBERS ARE UNIDIRECTIONAL, IN PAIRS, AS SHOWN BY ARROWS.
NOTE:- FORMER T.B. SERVICES NOW DISCONTINUED ARE SHOWN WITH PREFIX "X". (BY AUG 57)
J.C.GILLHAM
AUG 57 — 230
Cosham, Red Lion
NO ROUNDABOUT AT # UNTIL 5-8-57.
New road opened 2-9-57
J&K ran via Southampton Road & 6th Av until 1-9-57.
COSHAM Rly Stn.
At C.R.S., 19 on outside loop, 3 & 13 on inside
SOUTHBOUND DIRECT WIRE FROM # TO # REMOVED BY NOV 61.
PORTS CREEK
Hilsea Arches.
FROG REMOVED TO # BY 11·61
Southdown Garage No 2
Southdown Garage No 1, and Coach Station
TWO WIRES, NOT FOUR, 1934 to 1952
Coach & Horses
HILSEA
Authorised Trolleybus Extensions:- Along Havant Road to Rectory Avenue, Farlington; and Along Link Road and Allaway Avenue, via Paulsgrove Estate to Portchester Cross Road.
ORIGINAL LAYOUT UNTIL 20-6-42
Until Approx 1950
REVISED LAYOUT 21-6-42
ALL WIRES REMOVED BY NOV 61 FROM COMMERCIAL ROAD KINGSTON CRESCENT TWYFORD AVENUE GLADYS AVENUE NORTHERN PARADE AND THE JUNCTIONS OF THESE ROADS AT LANDPORT KINGSTON CROSS NORTH END AND HILSEA ARCHES
TIPNER
ALEXANDRA PARK
Depot See Inset
LAYOUT 1934 TO 1953
NORTH END
STUBBINGTON AVENUE
Authorised Trolleybus Extension
STAMSHAW
Kingston Cross
CHICHESTER ROAD
DISUSED BY NOV 61 BUT STILL INTACT
MILE END
BUCKLAND
COPNOR
Green Lane
North End Depot
SERVICE BAY
PAINT SHOP UNTIL 1932 & FROM 1957
Eastney Depot
BODY SHOP
COPNOR 1936 TO 1952
Authorised Trolleybus Extension to Stanley Ave.
KINGSTON
LANDPORT
Unicorn Gates
DOCKYARD Main Gate
PORTSEA
Portsmouth & Southsea Station
Guildhall
FRATTON
Fratton Station
Fratton Park Football Ground
MILTON "White House"
Fratton Bridge
Theatre Royal
Southdown Garage and Coach Station
Loop added approx 1941
Bradford Junction
Floating Bridge
POINT
Kings Road Junction
SOUTH-SEA
Sally Port
NEW LAYOUT BY 11·61
Pier Hotel
Havelock Park
LAYOUT 1936 TO 52
Depot, See Inset
ONLY SERVICES 3·4, 5·6, 7·8, 11·12, 17·18 STILL WORKING AT NOV 61.
IMPORTANT :- The Overhead Wire Layout shown here is as in Summer 1957, but the original layout of 1934-36 was exactly the same except where otherwise indicated, including the various quite complicated portions.
Entire System Re-surveyed by JCG Nov 61, and all found to be unchanged except where shown.
CLARENCE PIER
SOUTHDOWN ROUTE WORKED BY CORPORATION (INCLUDING ALSO THE 37A)
DOUBLE CURVE REMOVED IN OCT 54.
Festing Hotel
NO TURNING CIRCLE 1936 TO 1952, BUT DEPOT WIRES THE SAME.
EASTNEY
EAST SOUTHSEA
LAYOUT 1935 TO AT LEAST 1945
The Circle
The Strand
Southsea Common
STRAND-S.P.P.-FESTING HOTEL CLOSED 9-39, & REOPENED 20-6-42
Enquiry Bureau
Southsea Castle
31·40·41·42·45·45A 43·48·140·147 Terminus
SOUTH PARADE PIER

suggested a transport interchange at Cosham where buses could bring people from Leigh Park and Paulsgrove and they could then change to trolley buses.

In February, the Chamber of Trade prepared a report on the trolley bus question after investigating the department and interviewing officers. The conclusion was that the council's decision to abandon the system was right and on February 27, the council reaffirmed its decision.

Work started on the link road to Paulsgrove, now Southampton Road, in April. This created problems when the overhead wires had to be reslung at the roundabout near the Red Lion, Cosham. On the roundabout near the fire station at Cosham one of the original trolley standards is still hidden among the trees.

Mr. Simmonds presented his first report for the abandonment of the trolleys in September, 1958, but the committee rejected his report as being too severe. The proposal was to remove trolleys from three routes so only 16 trolley buses would be required. The alterations would save 200,000 miles and save some £18,000 a year. A second report, presented in October, was also rejected.

Eventually, in November, 1958, the city council agreed that consultants should be engaged. Their terms of reference were:

1. An examination of the present and future financial and economic aspects of the undertaking as a whole and of motor buses and trolley buses individually;
2. The making of any recommendations on any additions and withdrawals of motor buses or trolley buses, and equipment that may be necessary to provide the most economical undertaking consistent with an adequate service to the public;
3. The co-ordination agreement with Southdown Motor Services.

Harold Woodhead and Partners Ltd. was selected to carry out an in-depth study.

The work involved every aspect of the department, including assessment of all levels of staff and method and organisation of all duties. A lengthy study of painting buses was carried out with special emphasis on the painting of ceilings in the top deck. Until Formica and other plastics were introduced for ceilings, there was a serious problem with nicotine stains. The revised system of painting saved a significant amount of labour which, unfortunately, created redundancies. The co-ordination agreement was thoroughly studied, including all revenue and costs since 1946.

The consultants' report supported the General Manager's report that the trolley bus system should be abandoned. A recommendation that incentive schemes should be introduced for the workshop staff was rejected by the committee.

Between 1959 and 1965, 57 trolley buses would require major overhaul at a cost of £2,000 each. Passengers had declined by 11 per cent in two years, with the vast expansion in private car ownership and the consultants agreed there was no need for longer distance travel. All the points put forward by Mr. Simmons were supported by the consultants. The cost of this advice was 2,400 guineas for the report on the trolley bus system and co-ordination agreement and a similar sum for the general investigation. Mr. Simmons had done it for nothing.

The scene was now set for the ultimate abandonment of the system. Overhead equipment was removed as it became redundant. The scrap value of the entire system was estimated at £36,868. The entire overhead wire was cut up into 18-inch lengths and stored in boxes prior to disposal.

December 2, 1961, was the last day of trolley bus operation from North End depot. By then, all overhead wires in Victoria Road South and Northern Parade were removed. In April, 1962, the wire was removed from Guildhall Square.

The last day of any trolley bus operation was Saturday, July 27, 1963, fleet number 313 returning to Eastney depot via the 17/18 service. The 5/6 service was packed

Trolley bus 313 on the final journey into Eastney depot on July 27, 1963. A wreath was placed over the offside mirror by the Traffic Superintendent, Mr. A. Fielder. *(C.P.P.T.D.)*

with enthusiasts. No civic ceremony had been planned as happened for the trams. Number 313 arrived at 11.45 p.m. to be met by the Deputy Manager, Mr. Archie Fielder and an enthusiast provided a wreath which Mr. Fielder hung over the offside driving mirror. Thereby, ended 29 years of trolley bus operation — another milestone completed.

Life on the line

Mr. Ray Butler, now enjoying retirement, was one of the overhead linesmen in the 1950s. The linesman's job was to erect new overhead wire, attend to dewirements and carry out repairs when necessary during the night. At the control centre at Fratton Road there was a plan of the system with warning lights for each section. If a problem occurred, an overload relay would come into action, the operator then attempted to re-set the relay twice. If this failed to re-set, he would then call out Ray and his colleagues.

One Sunday Ray reported for duty at 2 p.m., hoping for a quiet shift. Before he took his coat off, a call came through — problems at Chichester Road/Copnor Road junction. As they went round the corner at Copnor Fire Station in the tower wagon, they were faced with overhead wires just 18 inches from the road surface. A trolley bus on its way north to Cosham caused the problem, or rather, the lack of communication between driver and conductor had. The conductor expected to go along Chichester Road so he operated the "frog" to switch the overhead to go left into Chichester Road but the bus driver was going north, resulting in the overhead boom and the bus parting company. The "fireworks display" from the wires shorting caused quite a scene. The team worked day and night to refix all the wires to have the system back in action for the Monday morning peak.

The normal bustle of traffic in the Guildhall Square was absent when this photograph was taken but the complex overhead wire system for the trolley buses is clearly visible.
(R. Butler)

Mystery of the missing hole

During the extension in Copnor Road, the overhead line foreman had several holes dug in the pavement to receive the trolley poles. As a crane had to be hired to lift the poles, it was necessary to lift paving stones, dig the hole, cover it with a large steel plate, then replace the paving stone until several holes had been made. One night, a man tripped over the paving stones and he then reported this to the police who called out the City Engineer's workmen. They lifted the paving stones, found the hole and filled it in. When the crane arrived later to fit the pole, the hole had disappeared.

Timber

In addition to carrying passengers, trolley buses have been used for other purposes, such as carrying timber and breaking up planks for firewood. Eddie Tanner, who was a driving instructor before he retired in 1981 recalls arriving at the Dockyard gates and seeing a trolley bus going up onto the pavement and rocking back and forwards. A large piece of driftwood was on the pavement, being broken up by the rear wheels. His driver found a piece of driftwood and earmarked it for a job at home. The plank was put into the lower saloon and while collecting fares, Eddie had a full-time occupation telling passengers not to trip over the plank.

Fireworks

Torrential rain on December 17, 1952, caused a mini "firework display" in Commercial Road. The 580-volt feeder was short circuited, flames three-feet high were seen and molten metal ran down the pole. Services were held up for a while and a shuttle service of buses was provided between North End and Sultan Road.

CHAPTER XI

ALL CHANGE

After the end of the Second World War, it was necessary to plan for the future. The bus fleet was ageing fast and the prospect of buying new vehicles was bleak. Except for the Bedfords and Daimlers, built to War Ministry specifications, the remainder of the vehicles was more than ten years old. The acute shortage of materials during the war had meant the engineering section operating on a "make do and mend" basis. A programme of rebuilding the wooden-framed Leylands of 1935/36 was started in the late-1940s and went on into the early 1950s. The department was allocated woodworking machinery still in use today.

The first post-war new bus was delivered in October, 1947, a Leyland chassis with a locally-built Reading body. Unfortunately, these bodies were not very successful as they were wooden framed of inferior, unseasoned timber, which proved a problem for the whole of their life.

A red letter day was April 10, 1948, when the office diary records that bus number 124, a Leyland T.D.4, was the first Portsmouth bus to complete 500,000 miles. Number 124 was converted to an open top during 1954 and ran on the seafront service until 1971. Owned by an enthusiast, the bus is still operational. The half million mile achievement was significant at the time, considering the conditions

The Leyland Titans were given an extra lease of life through major renovation during 1950. This "before and after" photograph shows the extent of work needed. (C.P.P.T.D.)

Fleet Number 200, a Leyland Titan P.D.1, was one of the first new post-war buses and its body was built by Readings in Portsmouth. It was withdrawn by 1964. *(C.P.P.T.D.)*

the vehicle under which the bus had operated. The engine had been overhauled several times during this mileage, as the technology associated with lubricating oils was not available 40 years ago. There are several Portsmouth buses running today which have completed half a million miles with original engines.

Further Crossleys delivered during 1948/49 had turbo transmissions, a form of automatic gearbox. The fluid flywheel was extremely troublesome and the engine unreliable, creating enormous problems for the engineers. In later years, the engines and gearboxes were removed from them and scrapped. Engines and gearboxes from the Leyland T.D.4s were overhauled and eventually fitted to the Crossleys and they became known as Leylandised Crossleys.

The peak for passengers carried and mileage operated was reached in 1948. During the financial year 1948/49, 7,861,434 miles were covered and 87,806,124 passengers were carried. An example of how busy the department was in this period

Readings, of Hilsea, Portsmouth, was the builder of the body of this Crossley DD 42/5T, fleet Number 13. *(J. Dorey)*

The engine and gearbox from Leyland Titan T.D.4s were used in fleet Number 48, which was new in 1949. It had a Crossley DD 42/7T chassis and Crossley body. *(G.H. Truran)*

Bus Number 190, one of the immediate post-war buses, a Leyland P.D.1 with w Weymann body. The engine fitted to the P.D.1 was originally developed for Army tanks. (J. Dorey)

Basic designs of bus were subtly altered by the different body-builders. This Leyland P.D.1, bus Number 3, was fitted with a Portsmouth-built Reading body. (P. Couper)

One of the most popular double-deckers ever built, the Leyland Titan Pd2/10 chassis with a Leyland body. This one, pictured in Southsea, is fleet Number 82. (G.H. Truran)

was the occasion of a cup tie at Fratton Park when Portsmouth played Newport County. A crowd of 48,000 supporters was cleared in 25 minutes by 33 double-deckers, 14 single-deckers and 19 trolley buses.

From then on, the decline started, with increased costs, the growth of car ownership and greater home entertainment contributing to a permanent effect on the viability of the department.

Throughout the whole of the department's existence, minor changes have been made to services and the frequency of operation. May 29, 1949, was a special occasion when the service from the Dockyard to Leigh Park started. As with other alterations, it was an extension of another service, in this instance the M/N route, from Rectory Avenue, Farlington, to Leigh Park. In June, 1955, this became the 148 route, later the number 16.

Service changes require a lot of effort from all sections of the department. New destination blinds have to be designed, manufactured and fitted, usually on a Sunday. Route furniture — bus stop poles, plates and passenger information — need to be installed. Administration makes adjustments for costing and calculating the change in mileage operated. Drivers need to be informed of changes and occasionally route training is necessary. When the former Southdown route 38 to Droxford was taken over in 1985, it was essential to show drivers the route.

The diary entry for September 27, 1953, records several service changes "giving a substantial reduction in mileage in view of adverse financial position."

During the deliberations to dispense with the trolley buses, long-term spending projections were made. A decision was made to buy all vehicles from revenue. In the past, all vehicles, trams and trolley lines had been bought by raising loans. The loan charges for trams were still being paid some eight years after they had been scrapped. As late as the 1960s, the department made provision for removing tramlines every year, allowing some £20,000 a year. When the trolley buses were scrapped, there was still an outstanding debt on the money borrowed to pay for the system.

From 1961, £60,000 a year was put into a renewals and reserve fund to finance the purchase of vehicles. By May, 1968, the Chairman was able to announce that the department was not one penny in the red and had reserves of £217,000. In spite of economies, such as one-man operation and reducing services, the annual reports each year reported a drop in passengers, on average, this has been two per cent. One report refers to the registration of new cars in Portsmouth, for example, in

The body of this Leyland Titan PD2/12, fleet Number 87, was by Metro Cammell. Six of this type were later converted to open-toppers. (G.H. Truran)

1951, about 1,000 were registered; less than ten years later, the figure was in the region of 15,000. In addition to the cars, there had been a large influx of motor-cycles.

Major restoration work was necessary on the Eastney and North End depots. The west wall at North End, now forming a boundary for the small estate of houses, was in danger of collapsing and repairs were carried out by the department's staff. Since 1929, residents of Methuen Road had complained about the noise from the Eastney depot. Buses travelling in the road and engines running in the early hours of the morning all created a nuisance. Letters sent to the *Evening News* before 1939 referrred to paying visitors due to stay a week leaving on the Tuesday morning because they could not sleep. The entrance, refuelling and bus washing machine were altered in 1963, improving the flow of vehicles in and out of the depot. In October, 1985, buses finally stopped using Methuen Road when the latest refuelling equipment and entrance were brought into use.

Increased costs and the difficulties of recruiting staff led to the introduction of one man operation — now known as one person operation. Drivers' and conductors' hours were unsociable with early turns starting around 4 a.m., late

A modern entrance at the rear of the depot, with access from Prince Albert Road, Eastney, was opened in October, 1985. *(Author)*

The original entrance to Eastney depot from Methuen Road, with its folding doors which were fitted in 1964. After October, 1986, the doors were for emergency use only. *(C.P.P.T.D.)*

"Space ships" was the nickname applied by staff to the Leyland Pd3/6 buses when these 64-seaters were refitted with 70 seats in 1963. Bus-number 125 had a M.C.W. body of 1959. *(P. Couper)*

THE LEYLAND TITAN AND TIGER CHASSIS

STARTING

BEFORE STARTING THE ENGINE

See that :

1. Radiator is full.
2. Engine oil level is correct (dipstick).
3. Fuel tank is full (gauge on side of tank) and fuel is turned on (tap on bulkhead immediately behind the injection pump).
4. Fuel pump and filter are primed.
5. Gear lever is in neutral.
6. Handbrake is **on.**
7. Engine stop control is in **run** position.

TO START THE ENGINE

1. Close the battery cut-off switch.
2. Move the starting switch to the **on** position.
3. Press the starter button firmly.
4. Release starter button as soon as the engine starts. Do not keep the starter running unduly long if the engine does not fire, but find the cause of the failure to start. It will sometimes be found necessary, especially during cold weather, to depress the accelerator pedal more or less fully for a few moments after the engine starts, but

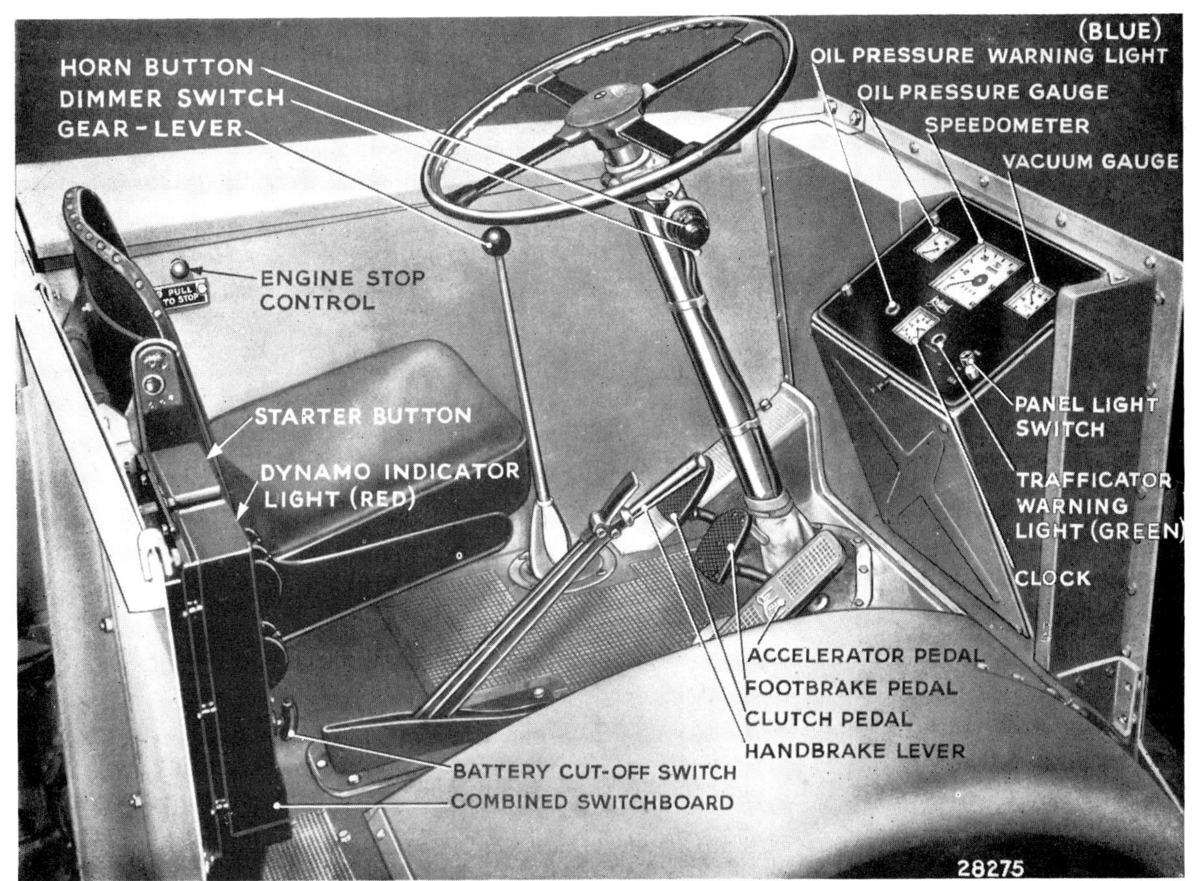

FIG. 4. DRIVER'S CONTROLS.

A Leyland Tiger Cub, bus Number 21, was bought in 1960 for the introduction of one-man operated services. It was withdrawn by 1973. *(P. Couper)*

A development of the Tiger Cub was the Leyland Leopard which was fitted with a larger engine. Bus Number 137 entered service in 1961 and the type was withdrawn by 1975. A later batch of Leopards remained in use until April, 1976. *(A. Lambert)*

Another redundant Corporation bus, Number 181, an A.E.C. Swift, was sold to a dealer in November, 1981. It is now run by an independent operator. *(A. Lambert)*

turns finishing after midnight and spreadovers starting around 6 a.m. and finishing in the early evening after three or four hours off in the middle. The spreadover shift was planned originally to cover morning and evening peak specials and the meal breaks of crews working early or late turns.

One-man buses had been operated in the 1920s with the Dennis single-deckers and up to 1939 on the seafront service using the Guy Runabouts. The Bedford O.W.B.s were modified so that the driver could open the passenger door from his seat. The first service operated by one person after the Second World War was from Hilsea Lido to Hillsley Road, Paulsgrove. Eventually, they were used on a service that became known as the Cosham Star Service, operating from Chatsworth Avenue, Highbury, to Wymering, back to Cosham and on to Troon Crescent, Drayton. In 1980, this service was used for an experimental flat fare of 10p. The increase in passengers was a success but it did not cover its costs.

The introduction of further one man services was marred with problems. The drivers, quite rightly, wanted more pay and discussions at national level took a long time to resolve. Other difficulties related to equipment and size and type of vehicle. In September and October, 1959, ten Leyland Tiger Cubs, equipped for one man operation were delivered, with approval for 34 seated and 26 standing passengers — a capacity almost the same as older double-deckers. Wage negotiations continued until a rate of drivers' pay plus 22 per cent. was agreed. The new single-deckers entered service in April, 1960, on the Highbury/Wymering and Hilsea/Paulsgrove services.

Over a ten-year period, several routes were one man operated during evenings and Sundays. Before 1968, double-deck vehicles were not allowed, by law, to be operated by one person, although London Transport experimented with closing the upper saloon of double-deckers during off-peak times and having drivers only.

The vehicle renewal programme was geared to take advantage of one person operation, with Leyland Panther Cubs and A.E.C. Swifts ordered. Leyland Atlanteans bought between 1963 and 1966, although not approved initially for one person use, were converted later, fleet number 201 being the first.

By July, 1979, all main routes, excluding the seafront service, were converted to one person operation. The seafront service was changed over from the summer of 1980 after the Traffic Commissioner had approved the route on a wet, windy day in February, 1980.

A similar AEC Swift with a Marshall body, bus Number 187, in the depot yard at Eastney. The red band on the coachwork was removed in 1979. All the AECs were withdrawn in November, 1981. *(G.H. Truran)*

A Leyland Panther Cub with a body by Marshall, of Cambridge, bus Number 157, pictured at The Hard, Portsea. A later batch, Numbers 162 - 175, were bodied by M.C.W. and entered service in 1967. All were withdrawn by 1981. *(G.H. Truran)*

One of the first double-deckers to be converted to one-person operation in 1971. Bus Number 201, an M.C.W.-bodied Leyland Atlantean, started service in 1963 and was withdrawn in 1975. *(P. Couper)*

A bus lending policy has continued occasionally since the Second World War. Bus Number 239, a Leyland Atlantean with an M.C.W. body, is shown on loan to Cardiff City Transport. It ended service in 1981. *(G.H. Truran)*

A Seddon Pennine body was mounted on a Leyland Atlantean chassis for bus Number 193 which began running in 1972. The last of the type to operate was Number 196 which was withdrawn in 1986. (G.H. Truran)

The 1968 Transport Act introduced the bus grant with the Government paying up to a quarter of the cost of a new bus, provided it was suitable for one person operation and operated more than half of its mileage on stage carriage services. From November, 1971, the grant was increased to 50 per cent. of the cost of a new vehicle.

The bus grant brought the introduction of sophisticated ticket issuing equipment but with electronic-assisted machinery in its infancy, there were numerous problems. One machine, the Videmat, printed a ticket that displayed an impression of the money tendered by passengers. It would even show washers and other flat items put into the machine. In spite of it being introduced to speed up the flow of passengers, the Videmat was short-lived. The latest machines issue a ticket with date, time, value, and the stage number where the pasenger boarded. By using a computer, a complete analysis of money taken and passengers carried is obtained from electronic equpment within the machine.

The increase in the volume of traffic during the early-1960s called for considerable management decisions. The traffic lights at the junction of Copnor Road and London Road at Hilsea created a serious bottleneck so it was decided to make a gyratory system around the Coach and Horses public house "island". A new concept, bus-only lanes, was also introduced. The London Road northbound bus-only lane opened in 1973 and during the construction of the M27 flyover and motorway works at Hilsea the short bus-only southbound lane was constructed. The lanes give bus drivers the chance to queue jump, helping them to maintain their timetables.

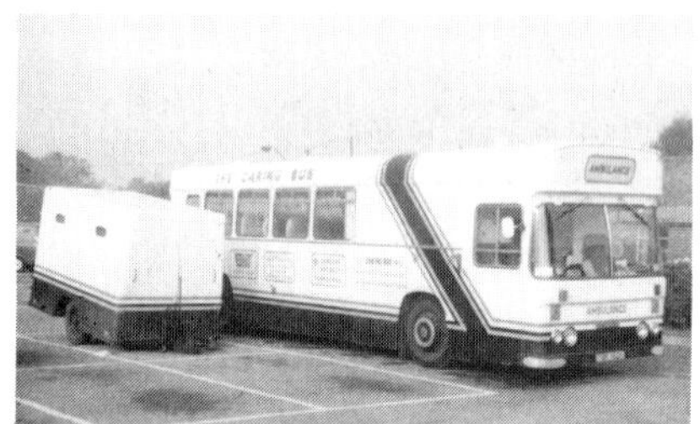

Former bus Number 192, a Leyland Atlantean bodied by Seddon Pennine, is owned by Mr. Phil Harris for charity work. The luggage trailer was bought by the Department from British Airways and sold with the bus.

Almost 30 years after the initial suggestion, a one-way system for Stamshaw Road (southbound) and Twyford Avenue (northbound) began in 1967. In the same year, an experimental pedestrian precinct started in Commercial Road between Lake Road and Arundel Street. During February and March, all traffic was banned and during April buses only were allowed. Despite desperate pleas by the transport operators, the precinct was made permanent in July, 1972. Services were diverted into Market Way, Unicorn Road and Edinburgh Road, so denying bus operators direct access to the shopping centre. The situation meant a longer walk to and from buses for shoppers and, regrettably for the bus, the car had better access.

Two other main roads in Portsmouth were improved after many years of creating problems for bus operators. Queen Street, Portsea, from the Dockyard to the city centre was so narrow in the early part of the century that the tramway was never

Still carrying passengers is former fleet Number 199, another Leyland Atlantean/Seddon Pennine, which is one of three owned by Portsmouth Ferry Port for transferring people to cross-Channel boats.

run there. For many years, the area was served with horse buses, then the motor bus in the early-1920s. After the devastation of the Second World War, the road was widened to its existing breadth. Arundel Street, Landport, caused many problems, too, as at one section it was so narrow that two buses could not pass. On one occasion, when a westbound driver disregarded instructions to wait for the eastbound bus the two became locked together and brought about the unplanned removal of a shop's sun blind.

On several occasions, Portsmouth buses have travelled across the water, with visits to France and the Isle of Wight. For the maiden voyage of a British Rail Sealink car ferry in August, 1961, three Corporation buses were taken to the Island. On their return journey, they carried civic dignitaries from the Isle of Wight to the Guildhall for a civic reception.

When the Continental Ferry Port was opened in June, 1976, an open-top Leyland P.D.2, fleet number 6, was taken to St.Malo to be the first vehicle off Brittany Ferries' ship Armorique. The bus was decorated all over with French and British flags and a variety of advertising material. The Thornycroft has made two visits to Le Havre since the ferry port has been open, one was a promotional exercise

Fleet Number 105, a Leyland National Mark I was delivered new in April, 1976. The author was fortunate to visit Leyland's factory at Workington in February, 1976, to see the 14 Leyland Nationals being built. (A. Lambert)

Two Leyland Nationals, a Mark I on the left (107) and a Mark II. All 14 of the Mark I type were withdrawn in November, 1981. Bus Number 100 had a dual purpose and was fitted with coach seats for private hire. It was transferred to Portsmouth City Transport. (C.P.P.T.D.)

The last double-decker vehicles bought by the Corporation were Leyland AN68 with bodies by East Lancashire Coachbuilders. They entered service in November, 1980, and were transferred to Portsmouth City Transport Limited in October, 1986. The bus pictured in Edinburgh Road is Number 346. (C.P.P.T.D.)

for departmental stores in Portsmouth and Le Havre. The author was on the second trip, a publicity visit for Townsend Thoresen ferries. Old Bill, as the Thornycroft is known, attracted a lot of attention from the French people but the journey from Le Havre to a superstore about eight miles away was somewhat trying for a 65-year-old bus. A line of traffic was held up through the tunnel out of Le Havre and on the return journey a long climb was too much, the radiator boiled, leaving a lot of rusty water on the Le Havre road.

Market research is carried out in many ways, usually by observations at bus stops, counting passengers boarding and alighting from buses. Head counts have been taken on buses when people have been employed on a casual basis to count passengers on buses. The most extensive survey of passenger movement started in September, 1981, and was known as MAP, Market Analysis Project, which was a system of analysing the travelling public's needs developed by a firm of consultants and the National Bus Company. The basis of the system was to divide the whole of the Portsmouth travel to work area into squares, with the size of the square determined by the level of population. Many questions were asked, such as: "Do you use the buses?" and "When did you last use the buses?" Visits were made to 1,000 homes in the city and people were employed to travel on buses and record where people were travelling. The results were then analysed to determine a schedule of routes and times of operation necessary to cover the requirements shown by the research.

Unfortunately, the MAP exercise had its unsavoury side as some staff were made redundant, 38 buses were no longer needed and North End depot was closed. November 1, 1981, was a sad day: from its peak in 1948, the size of the department's operation had been drastically reduced.

On an occasion in October, 1961, market research had its humorous side. Mr. Fielder had received requests to improve the service during the evening in Furze Lane, Milton. Mr. Fielder and an inspector made observations on two evenings. Later that week, the *Evening News* reported that two men had been seen lurking around streets and residents had contacted the police on the second night. The police visited the area and were about to apprehend the two when they discovered their identity. Fortunately, the inspector was a special constable and was able to identify himself and vouch for Mr. Fielder's presence.

When North End depot was closed in 1981 as an operational centre, memories of a previous plan to close the depot were recalled. In 1962, the Transport

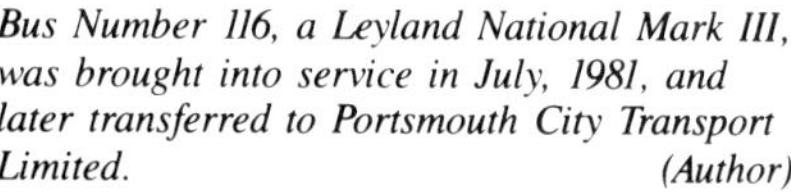

Bus Number 116, a Leyland National Mark III, was brought into service in July, 1981, and later transferred to Portsmouth City Transport Limited. (Author)

Committee considered relinquishing the site and moving to a purpose-built depot at Norway Road industrial estate, Hilsea. In December, 1962, after considering the financial implications, such as loan charges of £9,000, the committee decided not to go forward with the plan.

Mr. Simmonds retired in June, 1965, after seeing the department through the transitional period of the end of the trolley bus system, expansion to Leigh Park and the start of the one person operation. Mr. Fielder, who started working for the department as a conductor on the trams in 1924, was appointed General Manager. To the best of the author's knowledge, he is the only person in the passenger transport industry to start at the bottom and work his way to the top position of General Manager in the same undertaking. After an extension of service, Mr. Fielder retired in February, 1968.

Mr. Palmer, who was Traffic Superintendent, succeeded Mr. Fielder the following month but, unfortunately, he died in the following December. Mr. Dennis Racher, who had been appointed Deputy General Manager, became Acting Manager and Mr. Fielder came out of retirement to act in a consultancy capacity.

In 1969, Mr. Botterill, who had previously worked for the department as Commercial Officer, was appointed General Manager. Four years later, he became General Manager to Edinburgh City Transport, Mr. Racher then took over the post until his retirement in 1979. Mr. Boyes was appointed as General Manager, although the title changed to Passenger Transport Manager.

Throughout the 1960s, the department was able to show a trading profit. the annual reports for the years 1960/61 to 1969/70 show the trading profit as a percentage of working expenses declining from 11 per cent. to one per cent. Passengers reduced by some 12 million and mileage by one million. A clear indication of the further decline and very significant resistance to public transport. The oil crisis of the early 1970s was another heavy blow to all transport operations as massive increases in fuel costs had to be passed on to the passengers. On several occasions, it was necessary to raise fares twice in a financial year.

When the bus grant was introduced, operators placed large orders to replace their ailing fleets of vehicles and buy buses for one person operated services. The knock-on effect of the oil crisis was the high level of inflation and it became extremely difficult to budget for future revenue and capital spending. Placing orders for new vehicles was a nightmare. Suppliers had to include rise and fall clauses in their tenders; from the time of ordering to delivery a two-year gap was common.

The site of North End depot is marked by the small estate of homes on the west side of Gladys Avenue near the branch library. A horse tram depot had been on the land since about 1890. The later tram and bus depot was closed in November, 1981. *(Author)*

As part of a major fleet replacement programmed, 65 Leyland AN68s with bodies by Alexander were delivered between 1972 and 1975. This is bus Number 302. (G.H. Truran)

On one occasion, the price of a chassis rose from £11,892 to £17,413. The financial years of 1974 and 1975 saw a minus sign against the trading profit figure in the annual reports. This again called for further changes in the services, inevitably leading to reductions. In 20 years, the number of passengers carried had halved to 30 million and the mileage operated fell by 2,500,000.

The use of radio communication between the driver out on the road and the depot staff startd in 1974. There had been numerous incidents of attacks on drivers in other parts of the country, fortunately, no serious attack has ever occurred in Portsmouth. The opportunity for the driver to have instant contact with the depot and, consequently, the police is also a deterrent to vandals.

The Queen's Silver Jubilee of 1978 saw a massive influx of vehicles from National Bus companies throughout the South when over 100 vehicles were hired to provide a Park and Ride service for the weekend of the Fleet Review. Regretably, it was a costly exercise as the expected visitors did not arrive.

Rapid growth of the Continental Ferry Port gave rise to potential business and a double-decker was modified in the lower saloon. Seats were taken out and luggage racks fitted to one side to accommodate passengers travelling between the ferry port and Portsmouth Harbour Station.

Bus Number 330, a Leyland AN68 with Alexander body, was one of the vehicles (Numbers 320 to 344) fitted with fully-automatic gearchange and power steering. The driving cabs on this batch were updated with a design based on cabs being fitted to vehicles for Strathclyde P.T.E. at the same time by Alexanders. G.H. Truaran)

When British Rail Sealink introduced a service to the Channel Islands, there was a need to transport rail passengers and their luggage to the Ferry Port. Luggage trailers, which were redundant after their previous use on the London to Heathrow service, were bought from London Transport. After modifying the rear end of the single-deck Atlanteans, the operation commenced in the autumn of 1979. Within two years, they were replaced with double-deckers, the Walter Alexander-bodied A.N.68s, nine of which were modified in much the same way as the Atlanteans, their chassis being almost identical. They have proved to be very successful and operators in Poole and Dover have since made similar modifications to their buses, operating in the docks there. The 1972 Local Government Act gave powers to county councils to provide financial help to all public transport operators. They had powers to be involved in the co-ordination of public transport, including railways. Portsmouth received about 85,000 in the first operative financial year from April, 1974. The purpose was to give a subsidy to an operator to provide services which were unprofitable in their own right. The Portsmouth/Droxford route and others in rural areas were typical examples. The 1985 Transport Act removed from the county councils powers to coordinate transport.

The trend for advertising all over bus bodies which started in 1984, is illustrated by these Leyland AN68s, buses 332 and 338. (Author)

Bus Number 287 was painted to mark the fortieth anniversary of D-Day in 1984. Parts of the Operation Overload Tapestry, which is on display in the D-Day Museum, Southsea, are depicted on the side of the vehicle.
(E.C. Churchill)

Bus number 352 in all over advertisement.
(E.C. Churchill)

Improvements to depots and workshops also qualify for grants under the county transport policy. Several modifications at Eastney have been carried out with Hampshire County Council finance, the last major work being the new entrance to the depot from Prince Albert Road.

The Hard Interchange bus station at Portsea is a fine example of the county council being involved in co-ordinating three forms of public transport — buses and coaches, ferries from the Isle of Wight and Gosport, and the railway. The area around the Dockyard gates has been a terminal point for public transport since the days of the horse buses and trams. In trolley bus days, the overhead wire could accommodate three vehicles and it was a common occurence to see buses parked three abreast.

The concept of a purpose-built bus terminus was first considered in 1969. With local government reorganisation in 1974, the county council became the transport authority and was actively involved in pressing for a supplementary grant of over £1,000,000 to finance the scheme. Work started in August, 1977, when concrete piles were driven into clay beneath the mudflats and a concrete deck laid across. Lord Porchester conducted the official opening on Friday, May 18, 1979,

A Leyland AN68, bus Number 333, which entered service in January, 1979, is shown without the red band on its livery. It was in this area of the Eastney workshop that the bomb which caused so much damage fell in March, 1941. *(Author)*

accompanied by the Lord Mayor and other civic dignitaries. Special buses, including the old Thornycroft, took the guests to the Guildhall for lunch. One naval officer turned away his car and insisted on riding on the top deck of Old Bill.

Since 1974, the county has continued to provide subsidies for what are known as "socially-necessary services". Up to the 1985 Transport Act, the subsidy has been about £250,000. For the financial year ending March, 1980, Portsmouth City Council, after lengthy debates, agreed to provide a direct subsidy to the department from the rate fund. The maximum subsidy received from the council was £275,00, as with the county grant, this was for services which were unprofitable to operate, such as those on Sundays and evenings.

Bus Number 328 at The Hard Interchange, *now allows passengers easy transfer between buses, trains and ferries.* *(Author)*

Three trolley buses abreast outside the Dockyard gates shows the congestion caused at the terminus in The Hard. The overhead wires ran from three tracks into one, often leading to the dewirement of the outer trollery. *(L. Bern)*

Leigh Park Depot

After the extension of services to Leigh Park, it was decided to save dead mileage from Portsmouth by having a parking area in the district. On September 30, 1956, the office diary records: "Out parking of buses at Leigh Park commenced."

One of the Bedfords was altered to provide crew facilities, the main concern being a place for a cup of tea. It was not until the end of 1965 that the depot yard was concreted and purpose-built crew rooms set up. The depot, at Fulflood Road, has operated between 12 and 15 vehicles for many years. Southdown bases two vehicles there and the mobile library uses the site. The crews have always worked well together, the night men providing an early morning call for anyone who oversleeps. On his arrival at the depot, minus breakfast, the driver can look forward to at least a cup of tea. There have been instances where one driver has taken a bus out earlier than he should do so to cover for his mate who overslept. Some time later in the morning, they would swop over buses and continue with their own duties. Between them, the men can provide most D.I.Y. services for each other. The majority of crews live on the estate and, in some respects, have declared themselves independent of Eastney, giving a personalised service to the people of Leigh Park. Typical of their spirit and comradeship is that they have always organised their own social activities, such as dances and visits. From October 26th 1986 the depot became the operational centre for Portsmouth City Transport Limited's Private Hire operations.

No one loves a bus stop

The positioning of bus stops, shelters and termini has always created problems, people want to be near a bus route but no one wants a bus stop outside their house. One protest which ended in the Council Chamber occurred in 1952. The old G and H service terminated in Lovett Road, Copnor, and buses would stand outside one particular house for ten minutes or more with their engines running. It was reported that at one time up to seven buses would be in the road. Residents decided enough was enough and collected names of objectors and presented these to the General Manager but he rejected their plea. Eventually, councillors were called to observe what was going on and, after much discussion, the problem was overcome by moving the terminus.

It happened at Drayton

Ken Taylor, who now works at The Hard Interchange, was one of the first one-man operation drivers on the service from Cosham to Troon Crescent/Farlington Avenue. Driving to Troon Crescent one day, he saw a greengrocery van rolling down the hill with no driver. Ken jumped out of his bus, stopped the van and became a local hero. For several years after, whenever he was on that route and arrived at Troon Crescent at lunchtime, an admiral who lived near the terminus sent his maid to the bus with lunch for Ken on a silver tray.

The Bedfords had other jobs to do besides carrying passengers, for example, transporting a chicken coop. A driver was due to move house from the Eastney area to Paulsgrove so when he was working on a school special to Paulsgrove, travelling "dead" from Eastney, he arranged with his conductor to leave the depot early. They went round to the driver's house, collected the framework of his coop and a roll of chicken wire then loaded the whole lot into the rear of the Bedford. The schoolchildren were forbidden to ride in the back of the bus for the trip back to Paulsgrove.

There's something about a sailor

When the Portsmouth and Southsea "It's A Knockout" team won at Portsmouth in May, 1975, their prize was a trip to Nancy in France, in the July. Leyland Atlantean fleet number 311, at that time a new bus, was sent as a support vehicle for the team. The author was making his first visit to Portsmouth after appointment as Chief Engineer on July 14 when there was a minor panic in the office. The Lord Mayor was to have his photograph taken in front of the bus — with the destination blind showing Portsmouth Nancy. It was felt essential that the word "to" should be added between Portsmouth and Nancy.

CHAPTER XII

PORTSDOWN & HORNDEAN LIGHT RAILWAY

The principal organiser of public transport in Portsmouth, prior to the Corporation taking over, was the Provincial Tramways Company Ltd, operators of public transport in several large towns in England, which formed another company in 1897 to run a service from the city boundary to Horndean. Its formal title was Hampshire Light Railway (Electric) Ltd. but most people knew it as the Horndean Light Railway. The original intention was to take over the horse-drawn tramway from the boundary at the Green Post, Hilsea, electrify it to Cosham and eventually extend it to Horndean, following London Road through Purbrook, Waterlooville and Cowplain.

A Light Railway Order was applied for by the Provincial Tramways Company and an inquiry was held at Cosham on July 6, 1898. The original application contained a proposal to transfer goods from the railway on to purpose-built wagons and pull them on the tram track down to Portsmouth. The L. & S.W.R. objected to this, consequently the proposal was withdrawn. The company wanted to operate the tramway through Cosham High Street but, due to the narrow width in some sections, this was refused. The Order, or permission was granted in September, 1898.

Two of the horse-drawn buses which operated at the turn of the century between Cosham and Waterlooville are pictured with their conductors and other employees.
(C.H.T. Marshall)

Before Christmas, 1901, the Tramway Committee received a letter from a Mr. White, saying the Horndean Light Railway had appointed the council's Tramways Manager, Mr. E. Rotter, as its Engineer. Mr. Rotter had been in the post for less than a year and was involved in the planned electrification of the Corporation's system. With such a large commitment, there was a desperate need to have an experienced man in charge and a compromise was agreed eventually with Mr. Rotter retained as a consultant to the Corporation at £150 a year until the work was completed.

Construction of the line to Horndean began in 1901 and was open to the public on March 3, 1903. The service proved to be so popular that the following month five additional cars were ordered, making a total of 14 operating in the first year. Two further cars were to be delivered also.

The line to Horndean ran from a junction with the Corporation track opposite where the Portsbridge Hotel stands now at Cosham. Then across the fields to the east of the main road on the land where Roebuck House, the telephone exchange, police station and fire station are today. The route turned right,in front of the existing workshops for disabled people, over Southwick Hill Road and up Portsdown to

Staff of the Portsdown and Horndean Light Railway pose proudly in front of their vehicles. At the Companys depot at Cowplain. *(C.H.T. Marshall)*

Portsdown and Horndean Light Railway cars cross open fields west of Cosham village before climbing up Portsdown Hill on the skyline. *(C.H.T. Marshall)*

Site of the Portsdown and Horndean Light Railway on the side of Portsdown Hill. The stone steps alongside the A3 now lead to the housing estate. *(Author)*

the George public house. From there, it was single track with passing loops to Waterlooville in the main road, then on a roadside tramway on a grass verge from Hulbert Road. It was single track except for loops to the terminus at Horndean, just south of the Methodist chapel.

Numerous disputes between the company and the Corporation occurred over many years. Today, they would be considered petty but at the time both parties had significant investments to protect. Unfortunately, the lack of co-operation deprived residents of an excellent service from South Parade Pier through various points in Portsmouth to Horndean.

A major point of disagreement was the supply of power from Vivash Road to a metering point at Cosham opposite the Portsbridge Hotel. In 1901, the Hampshire Light Railway Company entered into an agreement with the Corporation for the supply of power at 2d per Board of Trade Unit, with a minimum of 250,000 units a year, for 21 years. A clause was included to protect the Corporation from any possible rise in the cost of coal and was implemented when the price was more than £1.10s (£1.50) a ton.

The footbridge over Southwick Hill Road at its junction with Portsdown Hill Road is all that remains of the light railway bridge. *(Author)*

Looking north towards the fairground on the sloped of Portsdown Hill with the Portsdown and Horndean Light Railway line in the foreground and and A3 road to London on the right. *(L. Bern)*

This well-known view of the top of Portsdown Hill shows tramcar Number 11 of the Portsdown and Horndean Light Railway on the extended loop at the crest. *(C.H.T. Marshall)*

Cars in storage at the Portsdown and Horndean Light Railway depot at Cowplain. A Waitrose supermarket now occupies the sight. *(C.H.T. Marshall)*

One other part of the agreement was to allow Portsmouth trams to travel on the company's track to an interchange platform known as Point A, opposite Widley Lane. Before 1907, Corporation trams had been allowed to the top of the hill, near the George inn. A Mr. Elkins, now in retirement, who was a tram driver for the company and later a bus conductor with Southdown, says that Point A can be found where the stone steps from London Road disappear into the bank.

The purchasing of power from Vivash Road proved very expensive; the company's bill for 1904/5 was more than £5,500 for operating 14 cars. The Corporation's costs for running 85 cars was considerably less than £5,000.

By July, 1907, the company had built its own power plant at Purbrook, using two diesel engines of 150 b.h.p. and two 100 kilowatts Brush Dynamos. On occasions, the company bought power from the Corporation, in April, 1916, and from December 8 to 11, 1929. In November, 1932, power was again supplied by the company, due to a fire at its own power station. In its original application, the company had wanted to use steam engines for pulling the cars but this was refused. A LIFU liquid fuel car was tried and at some time in the early-1900s ran in Portsmouth without success. It was used as an emergency breakdown vehicle but finished its days as a booking office outside the depot at Cowplain.

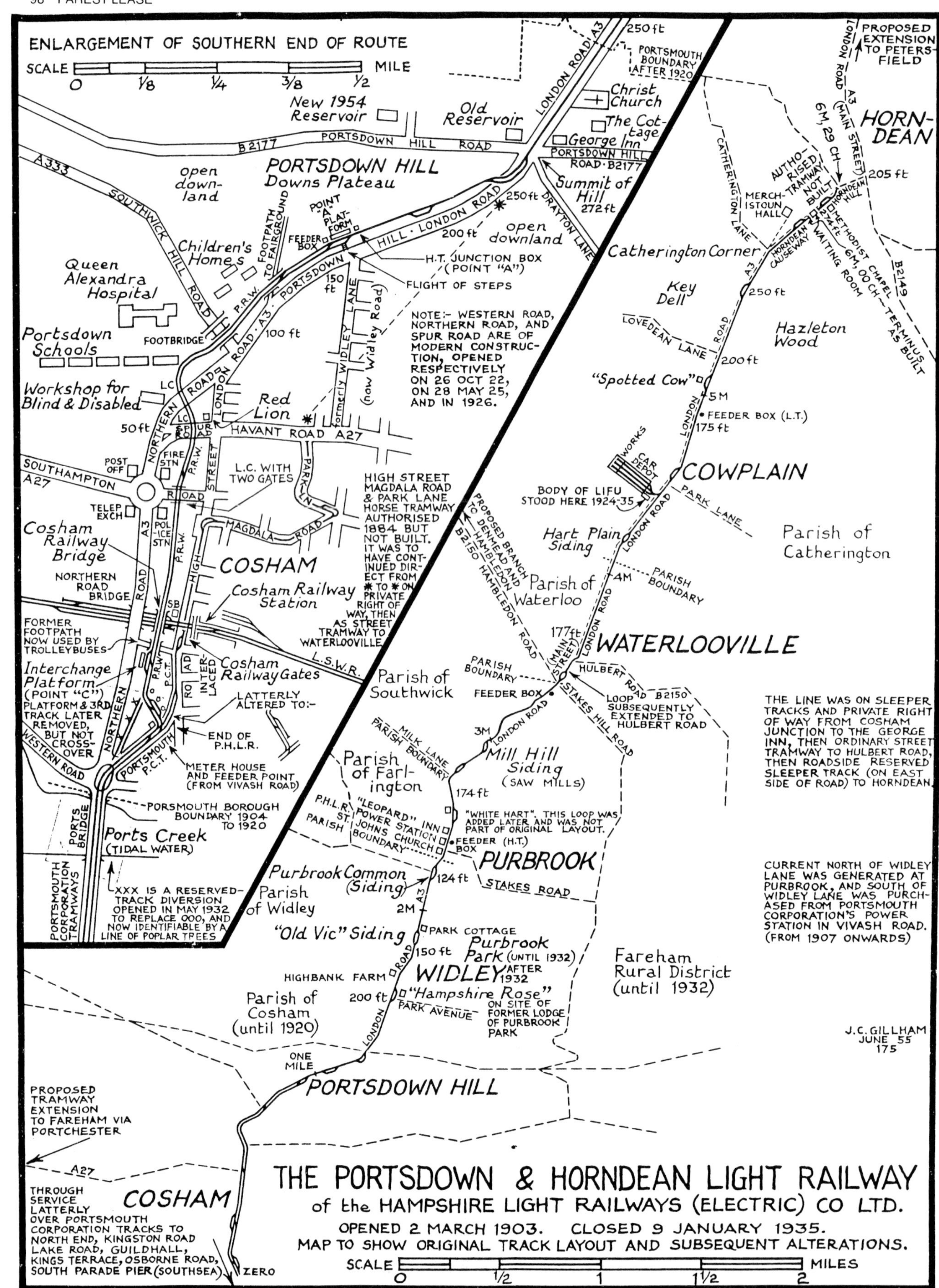
ENLARGEMENT OF SOUTHERN END OF ROUTE
SCALE 0 1/8 1/4 3/8 1/2 MILE
THE PORTSDOWN & HORNDEAN LIGHT RAILWAY
of the HAMPSHIRE LIGHT RAILWAYS (ELECTRIC) CO LTD.
OPENED 2 MARCH 1903. CLOSED 9 JANUARY 1935.
MAP TO SHOW ORIGINAL TRACK LAYOUT AND SUBSEQUENT ALTERATIONS.
SCALE 0 1/2 1 1 1/2 2 MILES
NOTE:- WESTERN ROAD, NORTHERN ROAD, AND SPUR ROAD ARE OF MODERN CONSTRUCTION, OPENED RESPECTIVELY ON 26 OCT 22, ON 28 MAY 25, AND IN 1926.
HIGH STREET MAGDALA ROAD & PARK LANE HORSE TRAMWAY AUTHORISED 1884 BUT NOT BUILT. IT WAS TO HAVE CONTINUED DIRECT FROM ✱ TO ✱ ON PRIVATE RIGHT OF WAY, THEN AS STREET TRAMWAY TO WATERLOOVILLE
XXX IS A RESERVED-TRACK DIVERSION OPENED IN MAY 1932 TO REPLACE OOO, AND NOW IDENTIFIABLE BY A LINE OF POPLAR TREES
THE LINE WAS ON SLEEPER TRACKS AND PRIVATE RIGHT OF WAY FROM COSHAM JUNCTION TO THE GEORGE INN, THEN ORDINARY STREET TRAMWAY TO HULBERT ROAD, THEN ROADSIDE RESERVED SLEEPER TRACK (ON EAST SIDE OF ROAD) TO HORNDEAN.
CURRENT NORTH OF WIDLEY LANE WAS GENERATED AT PURBROOK, AND SOUTH OF WIDLEY LANE WAS PURCHASED FROM PORTSMOUTH CORPORATION'S POWER STATION IN VIVASH ROAD. (FROM 1907 ONWARDS)
PROPOSED TRAMWAY EXTENSION TO FAREHAM VIA PORTCHESTER
THROUGH SERVICE LATTERLY OVER PORTSMOUTH CORPORATION TRACKS TO NORTH END, KINGSTON ROAD LAKE ROAD, GUILDHALL, KINGS TERRACE, OSBORNE ROAD, SOUTH PARADE PIER (SOUTHSEA)
PROPOSED EXTENSION TO PETERSFIELD
PROPOSED BRANCH TO DENMEAD AND HAMBLEDON
BODY OF LIFU STOOD HERE 1924-35
"WHITE HART". THIS LOOP WAS ADDED LATER AND WAS NOT PART OF ORIGINAL LAYOUT.
LOOP SUBSEQUENTLY EXTENDED TO HULBERT ROAD
AUTHORISED TRAMWAY NOT BUILT
6M, 00 CH - TERMINUS AS BUILT
6M, 29 CH
PORTSMOUTH BOUNDARY AFTER 1920
PORSMOUTH BOROUGH BOUNDARY 1904 TO 1920
Interchange Platform (POINT "C") PLATFORM & 3RD TRACK LATER REMOVED, BUT NOT CROSS-OVER
FORMER FOOTPATH NOW USED BY TROLLEYBUSES
METER HOUSE AND FEEDER POINT (FROM VIVASH ROAD)
H.T. JUNCTION BOX (POINT "A")
FLIGHT OF STEPS
LATTERLY ALTERED TO:-
END OF P.H.L.R.
PORTSDOWN HILL
Downs Plateau
COSHAM
HORNDEAN
COWPLAIN
WATERLOOVILLE
PURBROOK
WIDLEY
Catherington Corner
Parish of Catherington
Parish of Waterloo
Parish of Southwick
Parish of Farlington
Parish of Widley
Parish of Cosham (until 1920)
Fareham Rural District (until 1932)
Queen Alexandra Hospital
Portsdown Schools
Workshop for Blind & Disabled
Children's Homes
New 1954 Reservoir
Old Reservoir
Christ Church
The Cottage
George Inn
Summit of Hill 272 ft
Red Lion
Cosham Railway Station
Cosham Railway Bridge
Cosham Railway Gates
Ports Creek (TIDAL WATER)
PORTS BRIDGE
PORTSMOUTH CORPORATION TRAMWAYS
L.S.W.R.
"Spotted Cow"
Key Dell
Hazleton Wood
Hart Plain Siding
Mill Hill Siding (SAW MILLS)
"LEOPARD" INN
POWER STATION
ST. JOHNS CHURCH
Purbrook Common (Siding)
"Old Vic" Siding
Purbrook Park (UNTIL 1932)
HIGHBANK FARM
"Hampshire Rose" ON SITE OF FORMER LODGE OF PURBROOK PARK
PARK COTTAGE
ONE MILE
ZERO
J.C. GILLHAM JUNE 55 175

Portsdown and Horndean Light Railway.

LIST OF FARES.

1D.

Cosham & Widley Lane
Portsdown (The George) & Old Vicarage (Purbrook Pk.)
Old Vicarage (Purbrook Park) & Saw Mills
Saw Mills & Waterlooville (Havant Road)
Waterlooville (Havant Road) & Hartplain Avenue
Hartplain Avenue & Lovedean Road
Lovedean Road & Horndean

1½D.

Red Lion & Portsdown (The George)
Portsdown (The George) & Purbrook (The Leopard)
Purbrook (The Leopard) & Waterlooville (The Heroes)
Waterlooville (The Heroes) & Cowplain (Park Lane)
Cowplain (Park Lane) & Horndean

2D.

Cosham & Purbrook Park
Red Lion & Old Vicarage (Purbrook Park)
Portsdown (The George) & Saw Mills
Old Vicarage (Purbk. Pk.) & Waterlooville (Hav'nt Rd.)
Saw Mills & Cowplain (Park Lane)
Waterlooville (The Heroes) & Spotted Cow
Waterlooville (Havant Road) & Lovedean Road
Queen's Road & Horndean

3D.

Cosham & Saw Mills
Portsdown (The George) & Cowplain (Park Lane)
Saw Mills & Horndean

4D.

Cosham & Queen's Road
Red Lion & Cowplain (Park Lane)
Portsdown (The George) & Lovedean Road
Old Vicarage (Purbrook Park) & Horndean

5D.

Cosham & Cowplain (Spotted Cow)
Red Lion & Lovedean Road
Portsdown (The George) & Horndean

6D.

Cosham & Horndean

CHEAP DAY RETURN TICKETS BETWEEN COSHAM & HORNDEAN ISSUED ALL DAY 9D.

CHILDREN'S FARES.

Under 14 years of age
1d. for a 1d., 1½d. and 2d. Section
1½d. for a 3d. Section
2d. for a 4d. Section
3d. for 5d. and 6d. Section

School Tickets are issued for Children up to the age of 16 years travelling to and from School **only** between the hours of:

7.30 a.m. to 9.30 a.m.
12. 0 noon to 2. 0 p.m.
3.30 p.m. to 6. 0 p.m.

1d. for a 3d. Section
2d. for a 4d., 5d. and 6d. Section

Workmen's Cheap Return Tickets.

Are issued on all Cars up to, and including, the 8.5 a.m. from Horndean and the 8.15 a.m. from Cosham, as under :—

Cosham and Purbrook (Plant Lane) ... ... **3d.**
Portsdown (The George) and Queen's Rd., Waterlooville **3d.**
Purbrook Common & Cowplain Siding ... ... **3d.**
Waterlooville (Queen's Hotel) and Horndean ... ... **3d.**
Cosham & Cowplain Siding ... **4d.**
Portsdown (The George) and Horndean ... ... **4d.**
Cosham & Horndean ... ... **6d.**

Luggage under 28 lbs. carried free.

TRAMWAY OFFICES, GOSPORT.
October, 1928.

BY ORDER.

A typical Portsdown and Horndean Light Railway car, advertising two Portsmouth businesses, pictured at Cosham. (C. Phillips)

Soon after the line was opened, the company considered extensions, one to the new military hospital, now Queen Alexandra Hospital, and the other, more a wish of Mr. White, the General Manager, was to extend the track into Petersfield and then to Alton. They were granted permission but, due to the cost, did not proceed.

The line does not seem to have been a great commercial success, as in 1907, it was offered to the Corporation at cost plus 10 per cent. In 1926, Mr. Spaven had recommended to the Corporation Tramways Committee that it purchase the light railway. Joint operation had been considered several times and the company applied to the council to operate a through service, as it was concerned about competition from the Southdown Company and others.

The office diary gives the following information: "August 1, 1924, Horndean cars to Town Hall; December 15, 1924, Horndean cars to Palmerston Road, all drivers instructed by Inspector Flint; April 19, 1927, extended from Palmerston Road to South Parade Pier." Reference is made to the Horndean cars running to Clarence Pier on May 21, 1923, the *Evening News* refers to them as popular but there is no official confirmation of this.

Passengers on the Horndean cars running into Portsmouth were given two tickets for their journey to cover the respective sections, the company paying all the revenue taken in the city to the council, less working expenses. In April, 1930, the Transport Committee agreed to pay the light railway company £156 a year for clerical services, back-dated to July, 1929. The Corporation also agreed to make up the difference in the rates of pay between the company's and Corporation's employees, during the time they operated in Portsmouth.

When trolley bus operation started in Portsmouth in August, 1934, the writing was on the wall for the Horndean line. The company offered it to the Corporation but this was declined. The Southdown Company bought the line when it closed on January 9, 1935. The *Evening News* covered the event with letters to the Editor, photographs and editorials. Many correspondents expressed concern about what would happen to the employees. All found alternative employment, mainly with Southdown and some with the Corporation.

In a relatively short time, all the track and equipment was removed for scrap. Several of the tram car bodies were used as summer houses and one as a home in the Catherington area. Fortunately, three are in the possession of Portsmouth City Museums and, hopefully, one day will be displayed to the public.

This photograph of the light railway near the George public house at the top of Portsdown Hill marked the last day of operation. (The News, Portsmouth)

CHAPTER XIII

THE JOINT AGREEMENT

The Southdown Company started operating into Portsmouth before the First World War for a short period, due to fuel shortages, services were suspended until some time in 1919. Up to the Second World War, Southdown held a virtual monopoly over services north of Cosham railway gates. After the 1930 Traffic Act, the Corporation's General Manager, Mr. Hall, made several applications for licences to extend operations to Purbrook, Portchester and Rectory Avenue, Farlington, but the Traffic Commissioner refused on the grounds that the area was adequately served by Southdown.

The Corporation had had some success in restricting Southdown's activities in the city by imposing fare penalties through the Watch Committee, which granted licences before the 1930 Act. Many problems occurred with each operator accusing the other of devious moves to take away passengers.

Southdown bought out the Southsea Tourist Company which operated in Portsmouth, and took over the goodwill of the Portsdown and Horndean Light Railway. By obtaining these and other companies, Southdown gained a significant presence in the area surrounding the city, then during the Second World War, co-ordination had occurred through necessity and the Regional Transport Commissioners said it should be continued.

A form of co-ordination had been tried in the early-1930s. This agreement allowed Southdown to travel over tram routes at tram fares, the Corporation receiving all the money and paying Southdown a fixed sum for every mile it operated. The Corporation withdrew from this agreement after two years because it was losing money.

In 1945, the company had indicated its willingness to enter into a form of agreement. In a post-war situation, it was inevitable that city housing estates would have to be built beyond Cosham, such as at Paulsgrove. Mr. Hall pointed out that the principal advantages of an agreement would give a better service to the public. The need to change buses at Cosham and other points would be eliminated and such an agreement would give the Corporation authority to run beyond the city boundaries. It would also prove to be more economical, where fewer buses would be able to cope with the existing passengers.

A formal agreement was made in July, 1946,, following lengthy discussions between the managements of Southdown and the Corporation. Initial discussions started in May, 1945, and the operating area was defined as Petersfield to the north, Emsworth to the east, and Fareham to the west, an area of 127 square miles.

The total receipts and mileage for several previous years of both parties was collated, plus some estimating, to establish a formula. The final figures agreed were 57 per cent. to the Corporation and 43 per cent. to Southdown for both mileage and receipts. At the end of the war, the Corporation was suffering from an acute staff shortage and was unable to operate all its scheduled services so Southdown offered to operate any mileage the Corporation was unable to cover, at a price of 1s7d (8p) a mile. Negotiations went on up to the end of 1945 when Parliamentary approval was sought.

A referendum was held in the city, with 8,162 voting for the proposed Bill and 1,955 against. The voting paper gave clear statements on the proposed co-ordination agreement and was set out on a question and answer basis, such as, How can matters be changed?: 1) By purchasing the Southdown Company; 2) By selling the Corporation undertaking; 3) By seeking power to revive cut-throat competition; 4) By co-ordinating the services by sharing the territory of both undertakings in an orderly manner.

Before the agreement was signed, a firm of business consultants was engaged to vet it on behalf of the Corporation. They gave their approval that the agreement was fair and equitable to both sides.

The agreement commenced on July 1, 1946 for the financial year ending March 31, 1947, for 21 years. The first meeting of the Joint Committee, comprising officers and councillors for the Corporation and management of Southdown, was held on July 14, 1946, with Councillor H.E.Collins taking the chair. Joint secretaries were appointed, Mr. Peck for the Corporation and Mr. Hart for Southdown. The committee agreed to circulate to all staff a list of instructions regarding the co-ordination. The receipts from Southdown's famous 31 service to Brighton, regarded as the longest stage carriage route in the country, was also discussed.

The committee met quarterly, dealing with service changes, fare levels and every aspect of public transport in the desingated area. Up to the agreement being changed in 1967, it was a common occurence to see Corporation buses operating on Southdown routes and vice versa. The Bedford single-deckers were used frequently on the Hayling Island service because of the weight limit on the old bridge.

The agreement was due for renewal in March, 1967, although it could have been terminated at any time, provided both parties mutually agreed. After the revised agreement it could be terminated by either party giving twelve months notice. A mass of statistics was produced to justify continuing the agreement in a revised form, although the agreement did come under scrutiny in the 1950s when the Corporation called in consultants to review the Department. After the Market Analysis Project in 1981, the mileage proportion was set at 51 per cent. for the Corporation and 49 per cent. for Southdown because this had been the case for the previous three years.

There still are joint services, particularly those operating to Havant and Leigh Park but there are routes exclusively operated by Southdown to Waterlooville, Cowplain and other areas, which are defined as company routes.

Up to March 31, 1968, the fares received were aggregated and divided on the agreed percentage. After that date, each operator kept all the money it took except that three per cent of the difference between the amount Southdown received in the city and the amount the Corporation received on its services outside the city boundary would be handed over by the party which received the most.

The agreement came under scrutiny again when the Restrictive Trade Practices (Services) Order of 1976, following much political lobbying by the Municipal Transport Association, ruled that agreements between bus operators were excluded.

The 1985 Transport Act brought the joint agreement to an end. From 1968, Southdown had set the level of fares outside the city boundary and the Corporation those within the city. The Transport Act ended 40 years of close co-operation, reverting to the pre-war situation of open competition.

CHAPTER XIV

LIKE TO BE BESIDE THE SEASIDE

After a visit to Bournemouth in 1923, the Transport Committee decided to operate a special service along the seafront as a tourist attraction, using five novel vehicles known as Guy Runabouts. The service started on June 6, 1924, after due ceremony, when the Transport Committee was photographed with the vehicles.

Several private companies had operated a service along the seafront but none of them specifically for the holiday-makers. Southdown was running 60 day trips on a regular basis during the summer from South Parade Pier.

It can be assumed the service operated between the Hayling Island ferry terminal and Clarence Pier. The office diary for October 23, 1924, shows that the service operated between Clarence Pier and South Parade Pier only on Wednesdays. On October 26, the service was suspended.

The runabouts were the second batch of vehicles bought by the department. At that time, there was no depot at Eastney and temporary accommodation was found by using Milton Park Garage, at Hester Road, Milton, formerly used by the Southsea Tourist Company, at a rental of £1 a week.

For the summer of 1939, six single-decker Leyland Cheetahs with Wadham bodies and opening roofs were bought. During the summer of 1940, when the

The introduction of Guy Runabouts on the seafront service at Southsea was welcomed by members of the Tramways Committee in 1924. *(C.P.P.T.D.)*

On a sunny day the Runabout was popular with visitors and residents. Pneumatic tyres were fitted to the vehicles in 1929. (J. Dorey)

Leyland Cheetahs were bought in 1939 to replace the Guy Runabouts. Originally they were fitted with sunshine roofs by Wadham Brothers, of Waterlooville. (J. Dorey)

Open-topper fleet Number 8, a Leyland Titan T.D.4, was new in 1935. Originally fleet Number 125, it was converted for the seafront service in 1954 at Eastney depot workshops and finally withdrawn in 1972. It is owned by Portsmouth City Museums. (Author)

threat of invasion was looming, the seafront was put out of bounds and the service suspended for the remainder of the war. Three of the Cheetahs and one of the Guy Runabouts were destroyed during the air raid of March, 1941.

Between 1953 and 1955, four of a batch of Leyland Titan T.D.4s from 1935 were converted to open-toppers by removing the roof, fitting waterproof seat covers, and waterproofing the floor. For almost 20 years, they gave excellent service; all four are still in running order, three owned by enthusiasts and one by the City Museums.

Towards the end of their life, they proved a challenge to new drivers. The gearbox was a crash box type on all four forward gears and the cab was noisy and cramped, proving difficult to get in and out of round the large "push on" handbrake.

By 1972, they had been replaced by Leyland P.D.2s of 1956 vintage. The conversion was slightly more sophisticated in that a front shield was fitted and handrails fixed along the side of the top deck. The floor covering was the same as that used for the decks of yachts. All six are still in running order; one, fleet number 2, is still owned by the department and available for service and private hire. The others are owned by enthusiasts.

The paintwork scheme of Portsmouth buses has varied in the proportions of maroon and white. This Leyland PD4 open-topper is in the mainly-white livery. *(G.H. Truran)*

All of the open-toppers were converted from conventional buses. This Leyland T.D.4. fleet Number 125, was converted and renumbered 8. *(P.Couper)*

Open-top Leyland PD212, fleet Number 2, was fleet Number 100 before conversion in 1971. It was rebuilt in 1978 and is still is service for special events and private hire such as Derby Day outings to Epsom. *(Author)*

During 1981, the body of number 2 was extensively rebuilt by apprentices of the department. The bottom section of the main body pillars and the framework around the windows had become extensively corroded. The entire platform and staircase were rebuilt. Number 2 should now last for many years and, hopefully, one day will stand side by side with the Thornycroft and Leyland T.D.4 open-top in a museum.

During 1976/77, the Leyland P.D.2s were replaced with the present converted open-top Leyland Atlanteans. The financial need to move to one person operation called for a new specification. Due to several unfortunate incidents in other parts of the country where people had fallen over the side of open-top vehicles or been injured by a low bridge, Department of Transport vehicle inspectors laid down a stringent code of practice for open-top double-deckers which could be operated by one person. They insisted on having a side screen sufficiently high to prevent a child standing on a seat and falling over the side. The entire front screen on the top was retained to provide a windshield and the original periscope so that the driver can see people on the top deck from his seat was kept.

The seafront service now operates between Hayling Ferry and The Hard Interchange, providing a link between several attractions for visitors. They are used from the Spring Bank Holiday to the end of September, with a special day out to Epsom on the first Wednesday of June each year for Derby Day.

The latest open-top, a Leyland Atlantean suitable for one-person operation. Fleeet Number 10, pictured at the Hayling ferry terminus, was originally Number 252 and converted in 1978. *(Author)*

CHAPTER XV

SOCIAL LIFE

For many years, the Transport Department has had various forms of social activities organised by its employees.

The Tramways Social Athletic Sick and Benevolent Society started in February, 1923, by all members having 6d (2p) deducted from their pay. The objects of the society were: To provide benefits for sickness and accidents; To assist members in cases of exceptional distress; The promotion and encouragement of social activities and good fellowship between members. The principal activity now is to organise various sporting activities.

In December, 1926, the club was able to open new premises at Stubbington Avenue, North End, at the rear of what was White's furniture store (now Geldards). Later, the club moved to its present premises in Gamble Road, Buckland.

In its first annual report, for the year ending February 29, 1924, the activities of the society are detailed.

The Band. Originally formed in 1919, for many years concerts were given in Portsmouth, raising money for charity and its own fund.

Canteen. The canteen is still organised by the society with facilities provided by the department. It provides a variety of meals for crews during their meal breaks

Organisers of the Department's Benevolent Society posed for a photograph after their first meeting in Februrary, 1923, which laid the basis for the following years of welfare and social activities. *(C.P.P.T.D.)*

An impressive ceremony for the presentation of safe driving awards was held at the Town Hall in the early-1920s. The Transport Department band is in the foreground on the steps.
(C.P.P.T.D.)

— not that it is a case of chips with everything, except on Fridays when Hilda produces the best fish and chips in Portsmouth. The pinnacle of the year is the Christmas dinner with turkey and the usual trimmings.

Billiards and Snooker. The club was represented by several teams in various Portsmouth leagues and gave a good account of itself many times.

Whist. For many years the section met twice a week, providing entertainment for the men and their wives.

Rowing. Now the fishing section. Several excellent boats were kept in the club's boathouse in Bath Square, Old Portsmouth, still in regular use.

Rifle Club. In the 1923-24 season, Portsmouth Tramways won the local league, defeating other teams representing public houses.

Football. Without a doubt, the most popular section of the department. During April of every year, the Dupree Cup, provided by Portsmouth benefactor Sir William Dupree, is played for against Portsmouth Police. Fortunately, the event continues today, with supper provided by Whitbreads brewery. The large silver trophy, depicting scenes with the police and tramways staff working together, is said to be one of the most valuable sports trophies in existence. In recent years, the police have been more successful than the bus men. It was said for many years that a condition of having a job on the buses was the ability to play football. Any budding George Best was virtually guaranteed a job as an apprentice or points boy.

The Department's successful tug-of-war team pictured in 1925 with all its trophies. General Manager Mr. Spaven is in the centre.
(C.P.P.T.D.)

Water Polo. In the annual report it is recorded that some fine sport was enjoyed by all members.

Cricket. For a number of years friendly games were organised in the Portsmouth area and journeys by charabanc were often made to play against the Aldershot Traction Company, now Alder Valley, and the Southampton Tramways.

Social. This section continues to organise various outings, including those to end-of-season promotion matches to support Pompey in their efforts to seek promotion in the Football League. In the 1920s, evening drives at moderate fees were arranged. Concerts were run by the committee, with the artists being members and friends — there are a few "comics" on the staff today. Regular visits to pantomimes and trips to Brighton and Bournemouth are still made every year for the children of all employees.

Cycling. At the beginning, this section was very active but, no doubt, the increase in car ownership caused the decline of this section. It seems strange that after a week on the front of an open tram in inclement weather the men would want to spend their free time cycling in Hampshire.

Football has always been a popular social activity for staff and one of the best seasons was in 1936. General Manger Mr. Hall is to the left of the shield and Traffic Superintendent Mr. Prescott to the right. *(C.P.P.T.D.)*

The Mayor, Mr. J. Timpson, who was also Chairman of the Tramways Committee, shared the glory with the successful football team of 1919-20. *(C.P.P.T.D.)*

Darts. In recent years, a successful darts section has been created and teams regularly play as far afield as Great Yarmouth and Plymouth. In 1986, the section held several highly-successful fund-raising events, including a "bus-pull" from Eastney to The Hard, when the team pulled an open-top bus along the seafront. A 24-hour darts marathon, which raised money for a city hospital, established a world record for points scored.

In its first year, the total membership was 813 but it would now be impossible to achieve a membership of more than 350. Over many years, the society has carried out useful services, giving financial help to workmates who found themselves in difficulty, not least in the days before sick pay schemes in the 1920s. It was then a case of no work, no pay and many fell on hard times.

In its first report, the society records that assistance had been given following the death of one member and to five members who had lost their wives, with the total paid out amounting to £35. The Benevolent Section had done good work in giving aid to 21 cases. There had been an epidemic of influenza which had drawn substantially on funds. Over £132 was raised by a carnival dance for the Benevolent Society and a concert at the Town Hall raised a further £13.

Some 30 years later, the report for the year ending February, 1953, records a membership of 1,089, with a healthy financial situation, and notes the help given to alleviate distress among bus men and their families.

Into the 1960s, the society was known for the sports days and gala which were organised. The competition was always good and must have been an excellent way of improving morale and maintaining an excellent atmosphere among all the employees. Unfortunately, a fur and feather show held at the Wessex Drill Hall proved to be an utter failure.

The society continues to provide a social and beneficial need for all employees.

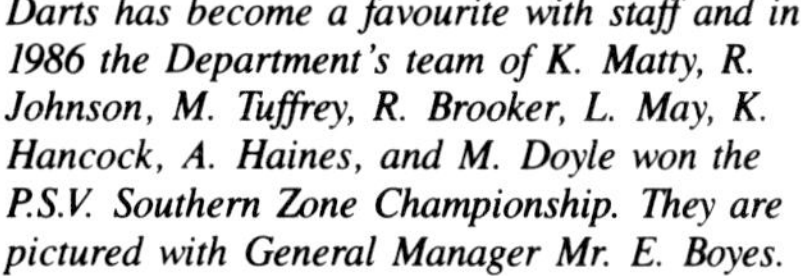

Darts has become a favourite with staff and in 1986 the Department's team of K. Matty, R. Johnson, M. Tuffrey, R. Brooker, L. May, K. Hancock, A. Haines, and M. Doyle won the P.S.V. Southern Zone Championship. They are pictured with General Manager Mr. E. Boyes.

CHAPTER XVI

OPEN ALL HOURS

Eastney Depot can almost be considered similar to the Windmill Theatre, at least in its motto — we never close. With the exception of Christmas Day, Boxing Day and New Year's Day, the depot is open 24 hours a day, seven days a week.

The first bus leaves the depot shortly before 4.30 a.m. and for this to happen the nightshift collects drivers and inspectors using a van. The nightshift starts at 11 p.m. when vehicles are cleaned and prepared for the next day. The shift also provides transport home for the drivers who have driven the last bus into the depot. At about 3 a.m., they go out again to collect drivers for the early buses. Between six and seven in the morning, the depot is a hive of activity with drivers signing on for duty, collecting all their equipment, and inspectors ensuring that the buses leave on time plus making arrangements to cover for drivers who fail to arrive due to sickness or oversleeping.

From 7 a.m., the dayshift takes over, when all major work on the vehicles is carried out, including preparation for the annual M.O.T. tests, bodywork maintenance and re-paints. Principal bus cleaning is done during the day and each bus receives a spring-clean about every six weeks. The evening shift takes over at 4 p.m. when every bus is refuelled, washed and swept in readiness for the following day.

The increasing size of the tram and bus fleet needed a purpose-built depot and work at Eastney, on the corner of Eastney Road and Highland Road, began in 1929. (C.P.P.T.D.)

The scale of the new depot can be gauged by comparison with the workmen in the foreground. At the back is one of the Foden steam wagons. *(C.P.P.T.D.)*

January 1, 1976, was the 75th birthday of the department. The 75th anniversary of the first tramcar operation on September 24 was marked by a special envelope with a first-day cover showing a line drawing of a tramcar of 1901 and a Leyland National bus of 1976.

To mark the occasion, an open day was arranged at the depot. Many sceptics said: "Who wants to look round a bus depot?", but over 1,000 did want to visit. Old vehicles were displayed including the trolley bus and Thornycroft, and a complete range of current vehicles. In the workshops, there was the opportunity to see where engines, gearboxes and many other items are repaired and a display of ticket equipment allowed children to issue tickets to themselves. Other open days have been held occasionally since, on the Saturday before the Vintage Transport Association's vehicle rally in June.

Bus Number 336, a Leyland AN68 with an Alexander body, which entered service in December, 1979, is shown before repainting when it was the last one to have the upper red band removed. It was transferred to Portsmouth City Transport Limited. (Author)

CHAPTER XVII

FROM P.C.T. AND BACK AGAIN

The forthcoming privatisation of the bus service led to a protest by Department staff in March, 1986, and a number formed a picket line at Eastney depot. (The News, Portsmouth)

In initials, the department has gone full circle from P.C.T., Portsmouth Corporation Tramways, to C.P.P.T.D. , City of Portsmouth Passenger Transport Department, and now from October 26, 1986, P.C.T., Portsmouth City Transport Limited.

The 1985 Transport Act started as a White Paper in July, 1984, the usual process of a Green Paper for discussion was by-passed. A mountain of paperwork was issued in the form of discussions for the passenger transport industry. In spite of intense lobbying, the Bill went through Parliament with only minor modifications.

On the day the Bill was published, the Secretary of State for Transport, Mr. Nicholas Ridley, was reported as saying: "The Transport Bill published today for the abolition of road service licensing in Great Britain outside London. This extends to local bus services the freedom from restrictions on competition which was so successfully introduced for express coach services in 1980.

The present system of regulation, which has been with us for 50 years, has stifled the flexibility and innovative approach which is necessary if the bus industry is to meet the travel needs of the 1980s. In the last ten years, fares went up by more than 30 per cent. faster than inflation, services declined and in some cases became virtually non-existent, yet revenue support for the bus services increased from £10 million in 1972 to over £500 million in 1985. This cycle of rising fares, rising costs and reducing services could not continue."

The scene was set for a considerable amount of head scratching and political debate. Officers of the department, the City Treasurers and City Secretariat spent many months preparing documents for consideration by the politicians.

Quite naturally, the trade unions involved were concerned as to how the Bill would affect the employment prospects of their members. The main worry was the security of everyone's pension as the Bill gave little assurance regarding the Local Government Superannuation Scheme. Portsmouth City Council decided to take up the "deeming option" so, at least for the foreseeable future, pensions appear to be safe.

The Transport and General Workers Union organised a national day of industrial action in November, 1985. This was the only occasion in the history of the department when the traffic and engineering staff withdrew 100 per cent. of their labour. Similar action, but for a Friday and following Monday, was planned for March, 1986, however, only a small number of staff were on strike on Friday and by the Monday everyone was working normally.

The new Act called for all operators to register with the Traffic Commissioners by February 28, 1986, what they considered to be a viable network of services. All other operators of buses and companies running lorries were encouraged by the Government to consider starting to run buses. By April, 1986, all registered services were published by the Traffic Commissioners. County councils were then in a position to assess the areas not covered by the registration process. These services were then put out to tender and any operator was able to quote how much

Private hire has become an increasing part of Portsmouth City Transport's services. Fleet Number 101, a Leyland Leopard chassis on a Duple-Dominant body is a 57-seat coach bought secondhand in May, 1986. (C.P.P.T.D.)

Towing vehicle fleet Number 480 was formerly a Leyland P.D.2 bus, fleet Number 114. The conversion was completed in the Department's workshop in April, 1976. The original crane was removed in November, 1985. (Author)

Eastney depot open day on October 18, 1986, when the public was invited to visit the depot for the introduction of Portsmouth City Transport Limited. *(Author)*

subsidy it would require to operate the tendered services. The tendering process required estimates to be made of possible income from those routes.

The department was fortunate in so far as it had information on what passenger loadings on the tendered routes had been and the operating costs in terms of pence per mile, making possible calculations for figures to be used in a tender.

By September, 1986, the department was informed of the routes it had been allocated under the tendering process. These were made up of early morning and late evening serices which the proposed company had not registered. Sunday services were not registered by the company but Southdown had registered several of the Corporation Sunday services. To make these potentially viable, Southdown added a premium to the Corporation fare structure which it also used.

The board of directors for the company was made up of three councillors from the ruling party, one from the majority opposition party and three executives who were former officers of the department. All were appointed and confirmed at a meeting of the City Council in October, 1985. A further three non-executive directors were appointed from outside the industry. A worker director was also appointed by a joint committee of the Trade Unions.

During 1986 several informal board meetings were held to discuss various policies for the proposed Company. On the 28th July 1986 the first formal board meeting was held at the Highland Road offices. Their first duty was to elect a chairman and Councillor F.A. Warner was duly elected as the first chairman of Portsmouth City Transport Ltd.

The first purpose-built recovery vehicle owned by the Department, and AEC Mandator with Dial Holmes 750 equipment, was bought by the Corporation in September, 1986. *(Author)*

FLEET LIST

PORTSMOUTH CORPORATION TRAMWAYS 1901 - 1936

Tram Cars

1 - 80 Truck: Brill
Bodybuilder and Equipment: Dick, Kerr 33/22
Entry into Service: 1901

81 - 84 Truck: Brill
Bodybuilder and Equipment: Milnes 26/20 with conversion from horse-tram to electric by Portsmouth Corporation in 1902
Entry into Service: 1880
Built at the North Metropolitan Works at Leytonstone and delivered as NEW to Portsmouth

Car 84 is preserved by Portsmouth City Museums, and in store at Eastney

85 - 100 Truck: Brill
Bodybuilder and Equipment: Dick, Kerr 32/22
Entry into Service 1906/7

101 - 103 Truck: Special
Bodybuilder and Equipment: Dick, Kerr
Entry into Service: 101 - 1903
102-103 - 1919

104 Truck: Brill
Bodybuilder and Equipment: Dick, Kerr 40
Entry into Service: 1919
Open-top toast rack and later fitted with a canopy.
New in 1900 and acquired from Southampton Corporation

105 - 116 Truck: Brill
Bodybuilder and Equipment: English Electric 36/22
Entry into Service: 1920
Closed-top cars

1 Truck: Peckham
Bodybuilder and Equipment: Portsmouth Corporation Tramways
Entry into Service: 1930
Seating: 35/23
Sold to Sunderland Tramways in 1936 and eventually withdrawn from service in 1953

LC 3378
1d
PORTSMOUTH CORP'N TRAMWAYS
Issued subject to conditions on Fare Bill. To be shown or given up on demand.
Dog
Luggage
1 2 3 4 5 6 7 8 9 10 11 12 13 14 15 16 17
18 19 20 21 22 23 24 25 26 27 28 29 30 31 32 33 34

CITY OF PORTSMOUTH PASSENGER TRANSPORT DEPARTMENT

Trolley Bus Fleet List 1934 to 1963

1 - 4
Chassis: A.E.C. 661T, built 1934
Body: English Electric H5OR
Equipment:English Electric

1 RV 4649 2 RV 4650 3 RV 4651 4 RV 4652

Renumbered 201 to 204 in 1938. Trolleybus 201 is preserved by Portsmouth City Museums in 1934 style livery, although with 'modern' style outlining

5 - 7
Chassis: Leyland TBD2, built 1934
Body: English Electric H5OR
Equipment: General Electrical Company

5 RV 4653 6 RV 4654 7 RV 4655

Renumbered 205 to 207 in 1938

8
Chassis:Sunbeam MF2, built 1934
Body: English Electric H5OR
Equipment: British Thompson-Houston

8 RV 4656

Renumbered 208 in 1938

9
Chassis: Karrier E4, built 1934
Body: English Electric H5OR
Equipment: English Electric

9 RV 4657

Renumbered 209 in 1938

10
Chassis: Sunbeam MF2, built 1934
Body:Metro-Cammell H5OR
Equipment: British Thompson-Houston

10 RV 4660

Renumbered 210 in 1938

11
Chassis: Karrier E4, built 1934
Body: Metro-Cammell H5OR
Equipment: British Thomspon-Houston

11 RV 4661

Renumbered 211 in 1934

12
Chassis: A.E.C. 661T, built 1934
Body: English Electric H6OR
Equipment: English Electric

12 RV 4658

Renumbered 212 in 1938
Three-axle vehicle

13
Chassis: Sunbeam MS3, built 1934
Body: English Electric H6OR
Equipment: British Thompson-Houston

13 RV 4659

Renumbered 213 in 1938
Three-axle vehicle

14 Chassis: Sunbeam MS3, built 1934
Body: Metro-Cammell H6OR
Equipment: English Electric

14 RV 4662

Renumbered 214 in 1938
Three-axle vehicle

15 Chassis: A.E.C. 663T, built 1934
Body: Metro-Cammell H6OR
Equipment: English Electric

15 RV 4663

Renumbered 215 in 1938
Three-axle vehicle

16 - 24 Chassis: A.E.C. 661T, built 1934
Body: English Electric H5OR
Equipment: English Electric

16	RV	6374	17	RV	6375	18	RV	6376	19	RV	6377	20	RV	6378
21	RV	6379	22	RV	6380	23	RV	6381	24	RV	6382			

Renumbered 216 to 224 in 1938

25 - 100 Chassis: A.E.C. 661T, built 1936 - 1937
Body: Craven H52R
Equipment: English Electric

25	RV	8307	26	RV	8308	27	RV	8309	28	RV	8310	29	RV	8311
30	RV	8312	31	RV	8313	32	RV	8314	33	RV	8315	34	RV	8316
35	RV	8317	36	RV	8318	37	RV	8319	38	RV	8320	39	RV	8321
40	RV	8322	41	RV	8323	42	RV	8324	43	RV	8325	44	RV	8326
45	RV	8327	46	RV	8328	47	RV	8329	48	RV	8330	49	RV	8331
50	RV	8332	51	RV	8333	52	RV	8334	53	RV	8335	54	RV	8336
55	RV	9106	56	RV	9107	57	RV	9108	58	RV	9109	59	RV	9110
60	RV	9111	61	RV	9112	62	RV	9113	63	RV	9114	64	RV	9115
65	RV	9116	66	RV	9117	67	RV	9118	68	RV	9119	69	RV	9120
70	RV	9121	71	RV	9122	72	RV	9123	73	RV	9124	74	RV	9125
75	RV	9126	76	RV	9127	77	RV	9128	78	RV	9129	79	RV	9130
80	RV	9131	81	RV	9132	82	RV	9133	83	RV	9134	84	RV	9135
85	RV	9136	86	RV	9137	87	RV	9138	88	RV	9139	89	RV	9140
90	RV	9141	91	RV	9142	92	RV	9143	93	RV	9144	94	RV	9145
95	RV	9149	96	RV	9150	97	RV	9151	98	RV	9152	99	RV	9153
100	RV	9154												

Renumbered 225 to 300 in 1938

301 - 315 Chassis: B.U.T. 9611T, built 1950/51
Body: Burlingham H52R
Equipment: English Electric

301 ERV	926	302 ERV	927	303 ERV	928	304 ERV	929	305 ERV	930
306 ERV	931	307 ERV	932	308 ERV	933	309 ERV	934	310 ERV	935
311 ERV	936	312 ERV	937	313 ERV	938	314 ERV	939	315 ERV	940

303 withdrawn from service in 1961 as a result of an accident. All other withdrawn at close of service on Saturday 27 July 1963, and stored until it was decided no buyer could be found. Trolley 313 is preserved by a private buyer.

Motor Bus Fleet List since 1919 **PORTSMOUTH CITY TRANSPORT**

1 - 10 Chassis:Thornycroft J, built 1919
Body: Wadhams 0334ROS

1	BK	2978	2	BK	2977	3	BK	2979	4	BK	2980	5	BK	2981
6	BK	2982	7	BK	2983	8	BK	2984	9	BK	2985	10	BK	2986

Buses still in service by 1927 were rebuilt with Dodson 'B' type bodies 034ROS (ex LGOC) and later converted to service lorries.
Number 10 is preserved by the Department, and renumbered 1

HALF-FARE NIPPERS
7/6 each.

11 - 15 Chassis: Guy J Type, built 1924
Body: Wadhams T15 (later reseated to 13)

11 TP 115 12 TP 116 13 TP 117 14 TP 118 15 TP 119

16 - 22 Chassis: Dennis 'Small', built 1924
Body:Stachen and Brown B20F (19-22: B25F)

16 TP 181 17 TP 182 18 TP 183 19 TP 186 20 TP 187
21 TP 188 22 TP 189

23 - 34 Chassis: Dennis 'Small', built 1925
Body: Dennis B26F

23 TP 751 24 TP 752 25 TP 753 26 TP 754 27 TP 755
28 TP 756 29 TP 757 30 TP 758 31 TP 759 32 TP 760
33 TP 761 34 TP 765

35 Chassis: A.E.C. 'B' Type, built 1925
Body: Dodson 034ROS

35 LF 9344

Ex: LGOC B2017

36 - 37 Chassis: Dennis 'E', built 1927
Body:Ransomes B32F

36 TP 4422 37 TP 4423

38 - 39 Chassis: Karrier CL6, built 1927
Body: Ransomes B32F

38 TP 4812 39 TP 4813

40 - 53 Chassis: Karrier WL6, built 1927/28
Body: Brush H6OR (48-53: English Electric H6OR)

40 TP 4703 41 TP 4704 42 TP 4705 43 TP 4832 44 TP 4833
45 TP 4834 46 TP 4835 47 TP 4836 48 TP 6872 49 TP 6873
50 TP 6874 51 TP 6875 52 TP 6876 53 TP 6877

54 - 61 Chassis: Dennis 'E', built 1928
Body: Davidson B32R

54 TP 6864 55 TP 6865 56 TP 6866 57 TP 6867 58 TP 6868
59 TP 6869 60 TP 6870 61 TP 6871

62 - 67 Chassis: Dennis EV, built 1929
Body: 62-65: Ben Lewis B32R
66-67 Portsmouth Commercial B32R

62 TP 8098 63 TP 8099 64 TP 8100 65 TP 8101 66 TP 8102
67 TP 8103

68 - 73 Chassis: Thornycroft BC Forward, built 1929
Body: 68-71: Ben Lewis B32R
72-73: Wadhams B32R

68 TP 8091 69 TP 8092 70 TP 8093 71 TP 8094 72 TP 8096
73 TP 8097

1 - 2 Chassis: Tilling-Stevens 'Express' B10A2, built 1932
Body: Park Royal B30R

1 RV 236 2 RV 237

3 Chassis: Leyland 'Lion' LT2, built 1932
Body: Park Royal B3OR

3 RV 238

4 - 10 Chassis: Leyland 'Titan' TD1, built 1930
Body: Short H5OR (7-8: Park Royal H5OR)

4 RV 241 5 RV 242 6 RV 243 7 RV 715 8 RV 716
9 RV 717 10 RV 718

35 Chassis: A.E.C. Regent I 661, built 1931
Body:Short H48R

35 RV 719

74 Chassis: Crossley Condor, built 1931
Body: Short H48R

74 RV 720

Preserved by Portsmouth City Museum. Converted to Breakdown Wagon in 1948

75 - 84 Chassis: Tilling-Stevens E60A6, built 1932
Body: English Electric H5OR

75 RV 1135 76 RV 1136 77 RV 1137 78 RV 1141 79 RV 1142
80 RV 1143 81 RV 1144 82 RV 1145 83 RV 1146 84 RV 1147

85 - 94 Chassis: Leyland Titan TD, built 1932
Body: English Electric H5OR

85 RV 1138 86 RV 1139 87 RV 1140 88 RV 1129 89 RV 1128
90 RV 1130 91 RV 1131 92 RV 1132 93 RV 1133 94 RV 1134

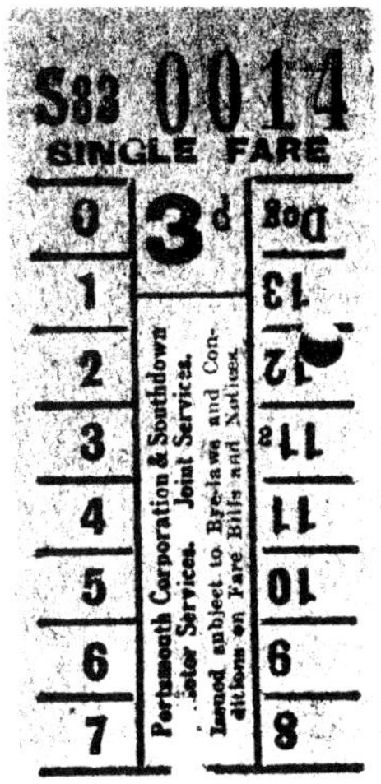

95 - 114 Chassis: Crossely Condor, built 1932
Body: English Electric H5OR

95 RV 1990 96 RV 1991 97 RV 1992 98 RV 1993 99 RV 1994
100 RV 1995 101 RV 1996 102 RV 1997 103 RV 1998 104 RV 1999
105 RV 2000 106 RV 2001 107 RV 2002 108 RV 2003 109 RV 2004
110 RV 2005 111 RV 2006 112 RV 2007 113 RV 2008 114 RV 2009

16 - 27 Chassis: Leyland Titan TD2, built 1933
Body: English Electric H5OR

16 RV 3410 17 RV 3411 18 RV 3412 19 RV 3413 20 RV 3414
21 RV 3415 22 RV 3416 23 RV 3417 24 RV 3418 25 RV 3419
26 RV 3420 27 RV 3421

17 and 18 converted to Tower Wagons in 1953 (TW1 and TW2) TW1 is preserved by Portsmouth City Museums

115 - 126 Chassis:Leyland Titan TD4, built 1935
Body: English Electric H5OR (126: H48R)

115 RV 6358 116 RV 6359 117 RV 6360 118 RV 6361 119 RV 6362
120 RV 6363 121 RV 6364 122 RV 6365 123 RV 6366 124 RV 6367
125 RV 6368 126 RV 6329

Buses 115, 117, 124, 125 converted to 050R (open-top) in 1953-1955, and renumbered 5, 6, 7, 8 respectively in 1959. No. 8 is preserved by Portsmouth City Museums and all other open-tops are in private ownership.

127 - 130 Chassis: Leyland Titan TD4, built 1935
Body: English Electric H52R
Purchased 1935. Sold 1942

127 RV 6370 128 RV 6371 129 RV 6372 130 RV 6373

129 withdrawn in 1958 and 127 renumbered 129 in 1959. Bus 130 was acquired for preservation by HCVC in 1962, but its whereabouts is not known.

52 Chassis: Daimler private car
Body: Limousine 7 seater

52 LG 522

Used on Highbury local service

131 - 160 Chassis: Leyland Titan TD4, built 1936
Body: Craven H5OR

131 RV 9385 132 RV 9386 133 RV 9387 134 RV 9388 135 RV 9389
136 RV 9390 137 RV 9391 138 RV 9392 139 RV 9393 140 RV 9394
141 RV 9395 142 RV 9396 143 RV 9397 144 RV 9398 145 RV 9399
146 RV 9400 147 RV 9401 148 RV 9402 149 RV 9403 150 RV 9404
151 RV 9405 152 RV 9406 153 RV 9407 154 RV 9408 155 RV 9409
156 RV 9410 157 RV 9411 158 RV 9412 159 RV 9413 160 RV 9424

41 - 46 Chassis: Leyland Cheetah LZ4, built 1939
Body: Wadhams B32C

41 BTP 941 42 BTP 942 43 BTP 943 44 BTP 944 45 BTP 945
46 BTP 946

41 and 42 destroyed by enemy action in 1941. Others withdrawn by 1955.

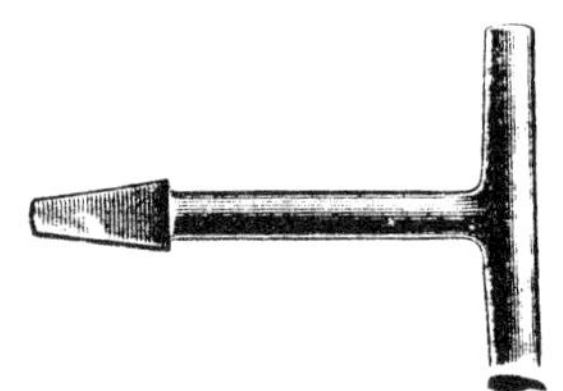

161 - 170 Chassis: Bedford OWB, built 1942 to 1944
Body: Duple B32F (162-163: Mulliner B32F)

161 CTP 3 162 CTP 19 163 CTP 41 164 CTP 85 165 CTP 86
166 CTP 87 167 CTP 88 168 CTP 89 169 CTP 199 170 CTP 200

Delivered with utility bodies and wooden-slatted seats. Reseated to B26F in 1955. 170 acquired for preservation in 1974, and more recently resold for preservation in 1981.

171 - 179 Chassis: Daimler CWA6, built 1944
Body: Duple H56R

171 CTP 151 172 CTP 152 173 CTP 167 174 CTP 175 175 CTP 176
176 CTP 177 177 CTP 178 178 CTP 179 179 CTP 180

Delivered with utility bodies and wooden-slatted seats, and in wartime grey livery. Rebodied to Crossley H56R in 1955.

199, 200, 1 - 4 Chassis:Leyland Titan PD1 or PD1A, built 1947/48
Body: Reading H52R

199 DTP 808 200 DTP 809 1 DTP 810 2 DTP 811 3 DTP 812
4 DTP 813

Bus 200 became a driver training bus, after withdrawal from regular service.

180 - 198 Chassis: Leyland Titan PD1 or PD1A, built 1948
Body: Weymann H56R

180 DTP 814 181 DTP 815 182 DTP 816 183 DTP 817 184 DTP 818
185 DTP 819 186 DTP 820 187 DTP 821 188 DTP 822 189 DTP 823
190 DTP 824 191 DTP 825 192 DTP 826 193 DRV 107 194 DRV 108
195 DRV 109 196 DRV 110 197 DRV 111 198 DRV 112

193 replaced bus 200 as Driver Training bus.

11 - 15/28 Chassis: Crossley DD42/5T, built 1948/49
Body: Reading H52R

11 EBK 23 12 EBK 24 13 EBK 25 14 EBK 26 15 EBK 27
28 EBK 28

29 - 42/47 - 57 Chassis: Crossley DD427T, built 1949
Body: Crossley H52R

29 EBK	566	30 EBK	567	31 EBK	568	32 EBK	569	33 EBK	570
34 EBK	571	35 EBK	572	36 EBK	573	37 EBK	574	38 EBK	575
39 EBK	576	40 EBK	577	41 EBK	578	42 EBK	579	47 EBK	580
48 EBK	581	49 EBK	582	50 EBK	583	51 EBK	584	52 EBK	585
53 EBK	586	54 EBK	587	55 EBK	588	56 EBK	589	57 EBK	590

Original Crossley engines replace with Leyland 8.6 litre type (from Cravens 131-160) reseated to H58R.

58 - 59 Chassis:Leyland Titan PD2/10, built 1952
Body:Leyland H56R

58 GTP	975	59 GTP	976	60 GTP	977	61 GTP	978	68 GTP	979
63 GTP	980	64 GTP	981	65 GTP	982	66 GTP	983	67 GTP	984
68 GTP	985	69 GTP	986	70 GTP	987	71 GTP	988	72 GTP	989
73 GTP	990	74 GTP	991	75 GTP	992	76 GTP	993	77 GTP	994
78 GTP	995	79 GTP	996	80 GTP	997	81 GTP	998	82 GTP	999

Buses 58 and 59 used on Driver Training duties (with 193) from May 1969.

83 - 107 Chassis:Leyland Titan PD2/12, built 1956
Body:Metro-Cammell H56R (reseated to H59R: 103: H6OR)

83 LRV	975	84 LRV	976	85 LRV	977	86 LRV	978	87 LRV	979
88 LRV	980	89 LRV	981	90 LRV	982	91 LRV	983	92 LRV	984
93 LRV	985	94 LRV	986	95 LRV	987	96 LRV	988	97 LRV	989
98 LRV	990	99 LRV	991	100 LRV	992	101 LRV	993	102 LRV	994
103 LRV	995	104 LRV	996	105 LRV	997	106 LRV	998	107 LRV	999

Bus 86 converted to Driver Training bus (replacing 193). Still in use during 1986. Painted in yellow and white livery.

Buses 99, 100, 103, 104, 94, 96 converted to open-top (1971 - 1972) and renumbered 1 to 6 respectively. All except No. 2 withdrawn by 1979 and all preserved under private ownership. No. 2 still in service during 1986. Nos. 90 and 92 used as Driver Training buses for a short while (replacing 58/59).

108 - 122 Chassis:Leyland PD2/40, built 1958
Body: Metro-Cammell H56R

108 ORV	985	109 ORV	986	110 ORV	987	111 ORV	988	112 ORV	989
113 ORV	990	114 ORV	991	115 ORV	992	116 ORV	993	117 ORV	994
118 ORV	995	119 ORV	996	120 ORV	997	121 ORV	998	122 ORV	999

All withdrawn by 1974. Bus 112 used as a Driver Training vehicle replacing 90. Eventually withdrawn (through accident damage) and is now preserved - but not repaired - by Portsmouth City Museums. Bus 114 converted to Breakdown Wagon to replace RV 720. Buses 111 and 115 were acquired for preservation.

123 - 127 Chassis:Leyland PD3/6, built 1959
Body: Metro-Cammell H64R

123 STP	995	124 STP	996	125 STP	997	126 STP	998	127 STP	999

Known as the 'Space ships' being the first 30′ length bus, although with front engine and rear (open) entrance. Reseated to H7OR in 1963, and withdrawn from service in 1974. Buses 123 and 127 sold to the Transport Road and Research Laboratories in 1975. Bus 125 on hire to Hants and Dorset in January 1975, and eventually returned to Portsmouth as a Driver Training bus replacing No. 92. Bus 126 used as a Driver Training vehicle from 1973.

16 - 25 Chassis: Leyland Tiger Cub PSUC1/1, built 1959
Body: Weymann B34D + 16

16 TTP	990	17 TTP	991	18 TTP	992	19 TTP	993	20 TTP	994
21 TTP	995	22 TTP	996	23 TTP	997	24 TTP	998	25 TTP	999

Delivered in maroon livery with white window surrounds. Six month's delay before introduced into service and repainted with white roofs, and reseated to B32D + 16. All withdrawn by 1974.

131 - 149 Chassis:Leyland Leopard L1, built 1961/1963
Body: Weymann B42D + 16 (143-149: B41D + 16)

131 YBK 131 132 YBK 132 133 YBK 133 134 YBK 134 135 YBK 135
136 YBK 136 137 YBK 137 138 YBK 138 139 YBK 139 140 YBK 140
141 YBK 141 142 YBK 142 143 143 BTP 144 144 BTP 145 145 BTP
146 146 BTP 147 147 BTP 148 148 BTP 149 149 BTP

Withdrawn 1974-1976. 148 converted to bus for the disabled and fitted with rear loading hydralic lift. Bus 147 used for a while as a Driver Training bus.

201 - 235 Chassis: Leyland Atlantean PDR1/1, built 1963
Body: Weymann H76F

201 201 BTP 202 202 BTP 203 203 BTP 204 204 BTP 205 205 BTP
206 206 BTP 207 207 BTP 208 208 BTP 209 209 BTP 210 210 BTP
211 211 BTP 212 212 BTP 213 213 BTP 214 214 BTP 215 215 BTP
216 216 BTP 217 217 BTP 218 218 BTP 219 219 BTP 220 220 BTP
221 221 BTP 222 222 BTP 223 223 BTP 224 224 BTP 225 225 BTP
226 226 CRV 227 227 CRV 228 228 CRV 229 229 CRV 230 230 CRV
231 231 CRV 232 232 CRV 233 233 CRV 234 234 CRV 235 235 CRV

202 converted to one man operation - first DD in the fleet. 201 to 230 eventually converted to OMO. Withdrawn between 1975 and 1978. 235 converted to Bus training and numbered LC77.

CONDUCTORS' CASH BAGS.

No. 1. **Price 11/-**

8-inches in depth by 10-inches in width, has two compartments, one having an expanding gusset of 1¼-inches. Complete with shoulder strap. A new feature of this pattern is the thin steel plate enclosed in the back, which preserves the shape.

236 - 245 Chassis:Leyland Atlantean PDR1/1, built 1964
Body: Metro-Cammell H76F

236 BBK 236B 237 BBK 237B 238 BBK 238B 239 BBK 239B 240 BBK 240B
241 BBK 214B 242 BBK 242B 243 BBK 243B 244 BBK 244B 245 BBK 245B

All converted to one-man operation. Bus 245 painted in all-over livery for McIlroys of Portsmouth in 1973.

246 - 254 Chassis:Leyland Atlantean PDR1/1, built 1966
Body: Metro-Cammell H76F

246 ERV 246D 247 ERV 247D 248 ERV 248D 249 ERV 249D 250 ERV 250D
251 ERV 215D 252 ERV 252D 253 ERV 253D 254 ERV 254D

All converted to one-man operation. Bus 249 painted in all-over livery for 'We're going to the Tricorn' in 1971. Buses 254, 249, 250, 252, 251 converted to open-top 1977-1979 - renumbered 7 to 11 respectively, still in service during 1986.

150 - 175 Chassis: Leyland Panther PSUR1/1, built 1967
Body: 150-161:Marshall B42D + 16
162-175: Metro-Cammell Weyman B42D + 16

150 GTP 150E 151 GTP 151E 152 GTP 152E 153 GTP 153E 154 GTP 154E
155 GTP 155E 156 GTP 156E 157 GTP 157E 158 GTP 158E 159 GTP 159E
160 GTP 160E 161 GTP 161E 162 GTP 162E 163 GTP 163E 164 GTP 164F
165 GTP 165F 166 GTP 166F 167 GTP 167F 168 GTP 168F 169 GTP 169F
170 GTP 170F 171 GTP 171F 172 GTP 172E 173 GTP 173F 174 GTP 174F
175 GTP 175F

Bus 172 delivered before August 1967, hence the 'E' registration. All withdrawn by November 1981.

176 - 187 Chassis: A.E.C. Swift built 1969
Body: Marshall B42D + 16

176 NTP 176H 177 NTP 177H 178 NTP 178H 179 NTP 179H 180 NTP 180H
181 NTP 181H 182 NTP 182H 183 NTP 183H 184 NTP 184H 185 NTP 185H
186 NTP 186H 187 NTP 187H

Bus 187 used a publicity bus for PORTSMOUTH MAP. All buses withdrawn after service on 31 October 1981 and have been sold to other operators/dealers.

188 - 199 Chassis: Leyland Atlantean PDR2/1, built 1971
Body: Seddon B4OD + 19

188 RTP 188J 189 RTP 189J 190 TBK 190L 191 TBK 191K 192 TBK 192K
193 TBK 193K 194 TBK 194K 195 TBK 195K 196 TBK 196K 197 TBK 197K
198 TBK 198K 199 TBK 199K

All except 189, 191, 193, 194 and 196 withdrawn from service by 31 October 1981, and sold. 197/199 have been retained for operation in the Continental Ferryport; 198 owned by Portsmouth Leisure Services and painted in a decorative livery and called 'Mavis'. 193 and 191 withdrawn 1/83 and 12/83 respectively. 193/194 cannibalized for scrap 1985. 189 to Hog's Lodge, Clanfield as static playbus; 191 to HMS Nelson.

255 - 272 Chassis: Leyland Atlantean AN68/1R, built 1972
Body: Alexander H75D + 5

255 VTP 255L 256 VTP 256L 257 VTP 257L 258 VTP 258L 259 VTP 259L
260 VTP 260L 261 VTP 261L 262 VTP 262L 263 VTP 263L 264 VTP 264L
265 VTP 265L 266 VTP 266L 267 VTP 267L 268 VTP 268L 269 VTP 269L
270 VTP 270L 271 VTP 271L 272 VTP 272L

All equipped for one-man operation. Colourbuses: 258: WH Smith (1979 - 1982); 262: Pleasurama (1980 - 1981); 266: The News, Portsmouth (1979 - 1982)

273 - 293 Chassis: Leyland Atlantean AN68/1R, built 1973
Body: Alexander H75D + 5

273 XTP 273L 264 XTP 274L 275 XTP 275L 276 XTP 276L 277 XTP 277L
278 XTP 278L 279 XTP 279L 280 XTP 280L 281 XTP 281L 282 XTP 282L
283 XTP 283L 284 XTP 284L 285 XTP 285L 286 XTP 286L 287 XTP 287L
288 XTP 288L 289 XTP 289L 290 XTP 290L 291 XTP 291L 292 XTP 292L
293 XTP 293L

All equippped for one-man operation. Bus 287 is fitted with two-way radio and PA System. Colourbus 274: Portsmouth City Lottery (1980-1981)

294 - 319 Chassis: Leyland Atlantean AN68/1R, built 1974/75
Body: Alexander H75D + 5

294 GOT 294N 295 GOT 295N 296 GOT 296N 297 GOT 297N 298 GOT 298N
299 GOT 299N 300 GOT 300N 301 GOT 301N 302 HOR 302N 303 HOR 303N
304 HOR 304N 305 HOR 305N 306 HOR 306N 307 HOR 307N 308 HOR 308N
309 HOR 309N 310 HOR 310N 311 HOR 311N 312 HOR 312N 313 HOR 313N
314 HOR 314N 315 HOR 315N 316 HOR 316N 317 HOR 317N 318 HOR 318N
319 HOR 319N

All equipped for one-man operation. Reseated for a while when fitted with Videmat Ticket Machines (loss of 1 seat). Buses 301 to 319 are fitted with two-way radios, and 311 has a PA System. Bus 311 sent to Nancy, France to publicise Portsmouth and Southsea with 'It's a Knockout' in July 1975.

104 - 114 Chassis: Leyland National 10351/2R B38D + 21 built 1976
Body:

101 KCR 101P 102 KCR 102P 103 KCR 103P 104 KCR 104P 105 KCR 105P
106 KCR 106P 107 KCR 107P 108 KCR 108P 109 KCR 109P 110 KCR 110P
111 KCR 111P 112 KCR 112P 113 KCR 113P 114 KCR 114P

All equipped for one-man operation and fitted with two-way radios. These were transferred to 301-319 when withdrawn from service after 31 October 1981.

320 - 334 Chassis:Leyland Atlantean AN68/1R built 1978
Body: Alexander H73D + 5

320 UOR 320T 321 UOR 321T 322 UOR 322T 323 UOR 323T 324 UOR 324T
325 UOR 325T 326 UOR 326T 327 UOR 327T 328 UOR 328T 329 UOR 329T
330 UOR 330T 331 UOR 331T 332 UOR 332T 333 UOR 333T 334 UOR 334T

All equipped for one-man operation and fitted with two way radios.

CONDUCTORS' CASH BAGS.

No. 2. **Price 8/6**

A new design just introduced. Has two compartments, rather smaller than No. 1, and made of the same good quality leather. Back measurements 9½-inches by 9½-inches. Also complete with shoulder strap.

335 - 344 Chassis:leyland Atlantean AN68/1R built 1979
Body: Alexander H73D + 5

335 YBK 335V 336 YBK 336V 337 YBK 337V 338 YBK 338V 339 YBK 339V
340 YBK 340V 341 YBK 341V 342 YBK 342V 343 YBK 343V 344 YBK 344V

All equipped for one-man operation and fitted with two-way radios.

98 - 100 Chassis: Leyland National 2 NL106L11/1R DP40F + 8 built 1980
Body:

98 CPO 98W 99 CPO 99W 100 CPO 100W

All equipped for one-man operation with two-way radios and PA System. Fitted with tachographs.

345 - 354 Chassis:Leyland Atlantean AN68A/1R built 1979
Body: East Lancs H73D + 5

345 CPO 345W 346 CPO 346W 347 CPO 347W 348 CPO 348W 349 CPO 349W
350 CPO 350W 351 CPO 351W 352 CPO 352W 353 CPO 353W 354 CPO 354W

All equipped for one-man operation and fitted with two-way radios and tachographs. Buses 346 and 350 have PA Systems fitted.

115 - 118 Chassis: Leyland National 2, built 1981
Body:

115 ERV 115W 116 ERV 116W 117 ERV 117W 118 ERV 118W

All equipped for one-man operation and fitted with two-way radios and tachographs. Bus 118 has the Gilton Illuminator destination equipment fitted.

95 - 97 Chassis: Dennis Lancet midi-bus, built 1981
Body: Wadham Stringer Vanguard B35F + 8 (95: DP33F + 8)

95 GTP 95X 96 GTP 96X 97 GTP 97X

All equipped for one-man operation and fitted with two-way radios and tachographs. Bus 95 has coach-type seats fitted.

101 Chassis: Leyland Leopard PSU5B/4R-43, built 1978
Body: Duple Dominant C57F

101 AUS 644S

Acquired from Stanley Hughes, dealers, of Yorkshire in May 1986. Former operator, Waddells Coaches of Lochwinnoch.

CHAIRMEN & GENERAL MANAGERS

Chairman of Tramways Committee

Councillor H. Kimber	1899 - 1907
Alderman Sir J.H. Corke	1908 - 1916
Alderman Sir John Timpson	1917 - 1936

Chairman of the Passenger Transport Committee

Alderman W.S.R. Pugsley	1937 - 1942
Councillor H. Lay	1942 - 1945
Alderman H.E. Collins	1945 - 1963
	1965 - 1968
Councillor W. Tooes	1964
Alderman C.W. Stevens	1968 - 1974

Chaiman of the Transportation Committee

Councillor G. Byng	1974 - 1983
Councillor S. Fiddy	1983 - to date

General Managers

E. Rotter	1899 - 1902
W.R. Spaven	1902 - 1926
Ben Hall	1926 - 1951
H.C. Simmonds	1951 - 1965
A.W. Fielder	1965 - 1968
R. Palmer	1968
R.E. Bottrill	1969 - 1973
D.I.C. Racher	1973 - 1979
E. Boyes B.A.	1979 - 1986

Chairman Portsmouth City Transport Limited

Councillor F.A. Warner Ch.Eng.M.I.E.E.	1986 - to date

TRAMWAY RE-CONSTRUCTION FROM 1920

Area Road	*Commenced*	*Completed*
Cosham Terminus		Opened 27th Feb 1920
Palmerston Road and circle	3.7.22 stopped	27.7.22
Osborne Road	3/11/22	14/12/22
Strand Road S.R.P.	14/12/22	1/2/23
Commercial Road All St. Church Crossover taken out at Sultan Road, and Air Balloon Rudmore Road, to Alexander Park		14/1/23
Reconstruction Commercial Road and Twyford Avenue, Greetham Street.		
Greetham Street	9/4/23	19/5/23
Kingston Cross and North End	9/4/23	17/5/23
North End Hilsea	24/5/23	
London Road between Ophir Road, Hilsea Avenue	22/10/23	9/12/23
Lake Road and Bradford Road	19/11/23	15/12/23 (Bradford Road only)
Lake Road Temporary arrangements	21/12/23	21/2/24
London Road (Copsey sidings)to Bapaume Road	21/1/24	20/1/24
All Saints Church, Charlotte Stree	7/3/24	31/3/24
Hilsea Avenue and Coach and Horses	10/3/24	2/4/24
Town Hall Victoria Hall	30/3/24	14/4/24
Bradford Junction,Victoria Road, Fratton Bridge and Havelock Road	28/4/24	26/5/24
Victoria Pier, Broad Street	12/5/24	8/6/24
Goldsmith Bridge	14/7/24	7/2/25
Pier Road between Pier Hotel and Clarence Pier	5/1/25	9/3/25
Cambridge Road and Grand Parade		
High Street	9/3/25	9/5/25
Victoria Hall Cambridge Junction	30/3/25	31/5/25
Cambridge Junction, Gun Wharf	29/4/25	31/5/25
New Road	17/6/25	15/9/25
Highland Road	1/10/25	11/12/25
Portsbridge Bapaume Road	24/11/25	11/12/25
Albert Road	6/1/26	10/3/26
Albert Road Police Station to Circle	10/3/26	29/4/26
Portsbridge, Bapume Road, Hilsea		
Bapaume Road to Cosham	7/3/26	15/4/26
Single Track		Double Track

Fawcett Road and Lawrence Road Tramway track removed 20/4/31.
Car service 13 - 14 terminated at junction of Rugby Road and Fawcett Road,
Fratton Bridge and Queens Hotel Service buses travelled via Goldsmith Avenue, Talbot Road, Fawcett Road, Albert Road and Waverley Road.
Fawcett Road reopened for traffic 7/7/31.
Clarence Road, Strand Circle 30/1/33
Fratton and Kingston Road, reconstruction and widening 27/6/34 commenced
3/8/34 Car service 9 - 10 withdrawn
1/10/34 Car service 7 - 8 Copnor Guildhall and Clarence Pier via Fratton Bridge withdrawn.
Car service 1 - 2 Cosham North End and Clarence Pier replaced by bus O and P to Red Lion
1/11/36 Trolley buses replaced trams on services 11 - 12 Copnor Bridge - Dockyard, service 15 - 16 Copnor Bridge - Floating Bridge. 10/11/36 Last tram 11.45 am from Guildhall to Eastney via Albert Road.

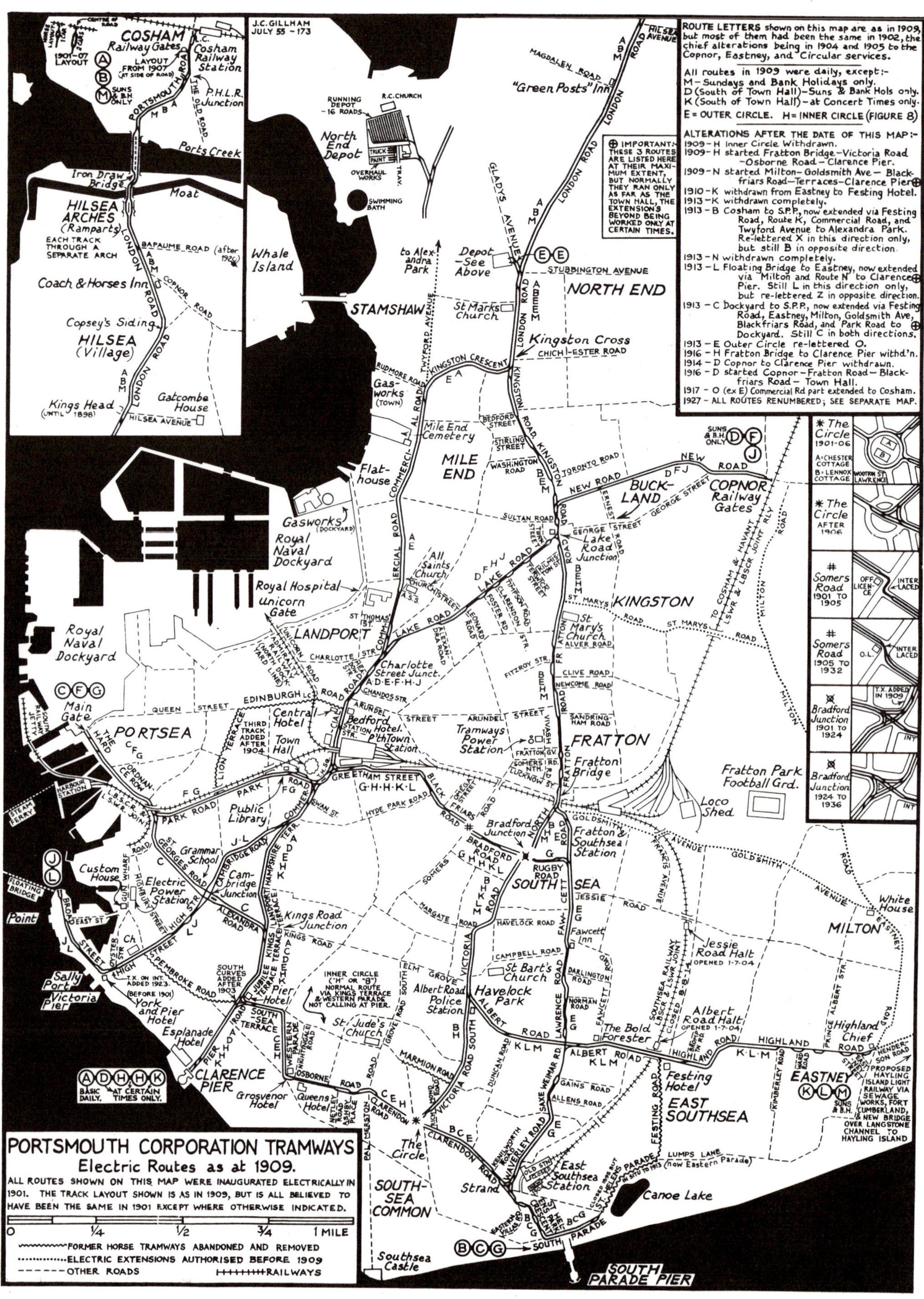

J.C. GILLHAM
JULY 55 - 173
ROUTE LETTERS shown on this map are as in 1909, but most of them had been the same in 1902, the chief alterations being in 1904 and 1905 to the Copnor, Eastney, and Circular services.
All routes in 1909 were daily, except:-
M - Sundays and Bank Holidays only.
D (South of Town Hall) - Suns & Bank Hols only.
K (South of Town Hall) - at Concert Times only.
E = OUTER CIRCLE. H = INNER CIRCLE (FIGURE 8)
ALTERATIONS AFTER THE DATE OF THIS MAP:-
1909 - H Inner Circle Withdrawn.
1909 - H started Fratton Bridge - Victoria Road - Osborne Road - Clarence Pier.
1909 - N started Milton - Goldsmith Ave - Blackfriars Road - Terraces - Clarence Pier ⊕
1910 - K withdrawn from Eastney to Festing Hotel.
1913 - K withdrawn completely.
1913 - B Cosham to S.P.P., now extended via Festing Road, Route K, Commercial Road, and Twyford Avenue to Alexandra Park. Re-lettered X in this direction only, but still B in opposite direction.
1913 - N withdrawn completely.
1913 - L Floating Bridge to Eastney, now extended via Milton and Route N to Clarence ⊕ Pier. Still L in this direction only, but re-lettered Z in opposite direction.
1913 - C Dockyard to S.P.P., now extended via Festing Road, Eastney, Milton, Goldsmith Ave, Blackfriars Road, and Park Road to ⊕ Dockyard. Still C in both directions.
1913 - E Outer Circle re-lettered O.
1916 - H Fratton Bridge to Clarence Pier withd'n.
1914 - D Copnor to Clarence Pier withdrawn.
1916 - D started Copnor - Fratton Road - Blackfriars Road - Town Hall.
1917 - O (ex E) Commercial Rd part extended to Cosham.
1927 - ALL ROUTES RENUMBERED; SEE SEPARATE MAP.
⊕ IMPORTANT: THESE 3 ROUTES ARE LISTED HERE AT THEIR MAXIMUM EXTENT, BUT NORMALLY THEY RAN ONLY AS FAR AS THE TOWN HALL, THE EXTENSIONS BEYOND BEING WORKED ONLY AT CERTAIN TIMES.
COSHAM
Railway Gates
Cosham Railway Station
1901-07 LAYOUT
LAYOUT FROM 1907 (AT SIDE OF ROAD)
SUNS & B.H. ONLY
P.H.L.R. Junction
Ports Creek
Iron Draw Bridge
Moat
HILSEA ARCHES (Ramparts)
EACH TRACK THROUGH A SEPARATE ARCH
BAPAUME ROAD (after 1920)
Coach & Horses Inn
COPNOR ROAD
Copsey's Siding
HILSEA (Village)
Kings Head (UNTIL 1898)
Gatcombe House
HILSEA AVENUE
LONDON ROAD
RUNNING DEPOT - 16 ROADS
R.C. CHURCH
North End Depot
OVERHAUL WORKS
SWIMMING BATH
Whale Island
to Alexandra Park
Depot - See Above
"Green Posts" Inn
MAGDALEN ROAD
HILSEA AVENUE
GLADYS AVENUE
STUBBINGTON AVENUE
NORTH END
STAMSHAW
St Marks Church
TWYFORD AVENUE
Kingston Cross
CHICHESTER ROAD
KINGSTON CRESCENT
RUDMORE ROAD
Gasworks (TOWN)
Mile End Cemetery
BEDFORD STREET
STIRLING STREET
WASHINGTON ROAD
MILE END
Flathouse
Gasworks (DOCKYARD)
Royal Naval Dockyard
Royal Hospital
Unicorn Gate
COMMERCIAL ROAD
All Saints Church
CHURCH STREET
LAKE ROAD
TORONTO ROAD
NEW ROAD
BUCKLAND
COPNOR Railway Gates
GEORGE STREET
SULTAN ROAD
Lake Road Junction
KINGSTON ROAD
KINGSTON
ST MARYS ROAD
St Mary's Church
ALVER ROAD
TO COSHAM & HAVANT LSWR & LBSCR JOINT RLY
MILTON
LANDPORT
ST THOMAS' ST.
CHARLOTTE STR.
Charlotte Street Junct. A·D·E·F·H·J
CHANDOS STR.
FITZROY STR.
CLIVE ROAD
NEWCOME ROAD
SANDRINGHAM ROAD
Royal Naval Dockyard
Main Gate
QUEEN STREET
EDINBURGH ROAD
ARUNDEL STREET
Central Hotel
Bedford Hotel
Town Hall
P'th Town Station
THIRD TRACK ADDED AFTER 1904
LION TERRACE
PORTSEA
THE HARD
Tramways Power Station
FRATTON
Fratton Bridge
FRATTON ROAD
Fratton Park Football Grd.
Loco Shed
GREETHAM STREET
G·H·H·K·L
BLACKFRIARS ROAD
HYDE PARK ROAD
PARK ROAD
Public Library
HARBOUR STATION
L.B.S.C.R. L.S.W.R. JOINT
STEAM FERRY
Bradford Junction
FRATTON & Southsea Station
GOLDSMITH AVENUE
FRANCIS AVENUE
Grammar School
Custom House
Electric Power Station
Cambridge Junction
ALEXANDRA ROAD
HAMPSHIRE TERR.
FLOATING BRIDGE
Point
EAST ST.
BROAD STREET
HIGH STREET
OYSTER STR.
Kings Road Junction
KINGS ROAD
MARGATE ROAD
RUGBY ROAD
SOUTHSEA
JESSIE ROAD
HAVELOCK ROAD
Fawcett Inn
Jessie Road Halt OPENED 1-7-04
White House
MILTON
EASTNEY
Sally Port
Victoria Pier
T.X. ON INT. ADDED 1923.
(BEFORE 1901)
York and Pier Hotel
PEMBROKE ROAD
SOUTH CURVES ADDED AFTER 1903
INNER CIRCLE ("H" OR "8") NORMAL ROUTE VIA KINGS TERRACE & WESTERN PARADE NOT CALLING AT PIER.
ELM GROVE
CAMPBELL ROAD
St Bart's Church
Havelock Park
DARLINGTON ROAD
NORMAN ROAD
Albert Road Police Station
Esplanade Hotel
Pier Hotel
St Jude's Church
ALBERT ROAD
The Bold Forester
Albert Road Halt OPENED 1-7-04
SOUTHSEA RAILWAY LBSCR & LSWR JOINT CLOSED 8-8-14
HIGHLAND ROAD
Highland Chief
PRINCE ALBERT STR.
KIMBERLEY ROAD
HENDERSON ROAD
PROPOSED HAYLING ISLAND LIGHT RAILWAY VIA SEWAGE WORKS, FORT CUMBERLAND, & NEW BRIDGE OVER LANGSTONE CHANNEL TO HAYLING ISLAND
CLARENCE PIER
Grosvenor Hotel
Queens Hotel
OSBORNE ROAD
MARMION ROAD
CLARENDON ROAD
The Circle
Festing Hotel
EAST SOUTHSEA
FESTING ROAD
GAINS ROAD
ALLENS ROAD
WAVERLEY ROAD
St. HELENS PARADE
LUMPS LANE (now Eastern Parade)
East Southsea Station
Strand
SOUTHSEA COMMON
Canoe Lake
SOUTH PARADE
SOUTH PARADE PIER
Southsea Castle
BASIC DAILY.
AT CERTAIN TIMES ONLY.
SUNS & B.H. ONLY
The Circle 1901-06
A: CHESTER COTTAGE
B: LENNOX COTTAGE
The Circle AFTER 1906
Somers Road 1901 TO 1905
OFF LICENCE
INTERLACED
Somers Road 1905 TO 1932
Bradford Junction 1901 TO 1924
T.X. ADDED IN 1909
Bradford Junction 1924 TO 1936
PORTSMOUTH CORPORATION TRAMWAYS
Electric Routes as at 1909.
ALL ROUTES SHOWN ON THIS MAP WERE INAUGURATED ELECTRICALLY IN 1901. THE TRACK LAYOUT SHOWN IS AS IN 1909, BUT IS ALL BELIEVED TO HAVE BEEN THE SAME IN 1901 EXCEPT WHERE OTHERWISE INDICATED.
0 1/4 1/2 3/4 1 MILE
FORMER HORSE TRAMWAYS ABANDONED AND REMOVED
ELECTRIC EXTENSIONS AUTHORISED BEFORE 1909
OTHER ROADS
RAILWAYS